Altogether Lovely:

Jonathan Edwards on the Glory and Excellency of Jesus Christ

Collected and Edited by Dr. Don Kistler

Soli Deo Gloria Publications
. . . for instruction in righteousness . . .

Soli Deo Gloria Publications
A division of Soli Deo Gloria Ministries, Inc.
P. O. Box 451, Morgan, PA 15064
(412) 221-1901/FAX 221-1902
www.SDGbooks.com

*

Altogether Lovely: Jonathan Edwards on the Glory and Excellency of Jesus Christ is © 1997 by Soli Deo Gloria. Printed in the U.S.A. All rights reserved.

*

ISBN 1-57358-071-6

Contents

Foreword by R. C. Sproul	iv
God the Best Portion of the Christian *Preached in April, 1736*	1
The Excellency of Christ *Preached in August, 1736*	14
Christ Exalted *Preached in August, 1738*	59
Safety, Fullness, and Sweet Refreshment in Christ *Preached in August, 1736*	79
Jesus Christ the Same Yesterday, Today, and Forever *Preached in April, 1738*	114
The Pure in Heart Blessed *Preached in Stockbridge, MA in 1753*	140
Christ the Example of Ministers *An ordination sermon preached on June 28, 1749*	176
Unbelievers Condemn the Glory and Excellency of Christ *Preached in May, 1736*	198
Praise One of the Chief Employments of Heaven *Preached on November 7, 1734*	211

Foreword

In my responsibilities as a professor of Systematic Theology, I have the opportunity at times to select elective courses of my own choosing to teach. One of my favorite such courses is "The Theology Of Jonathan Edwards As Seen In His Sermons." The study of sermonic material is not usually undertaken in the context of theology courses. But the sermons of Edwards are so rich in theological content that they merit inclusion in a theological curriculum.

Edwards's theological writings, such as *The Freedom of the Will,* or *A Treatise on Original Sin,* and even *The Religious Affections,* can be intellectually intimidating, even to seminary students. His work is so profound and so precise as to be demanding even to the most acute thinker. When we canvas the magisterial teachers God has given to the church throughout the ages we may be in awe at the prodigious display of knowledge and acumen they manifest. Calvin's knowledge of the Bible and of the church Fathers was encyclopedic in scope. Luther's insights into various vignettes of Scripture were uncanny. Turretine's systematic grasp of the entire scope of theology was awe-inspiring. But when we consider the sheer power of intellect, the native brilliance of mind, and the depth of ratiocination, three thinkers reach the acme of thought in church history. They are Aurelius Augustine, Thomas Aquinas, and Jonathan Edwards. Augustine has been esteemed as the greatest thinker of the first millennium of Christian history. Those who followed him had the advantage of standing on his shoulders.

In my judgment, however, the two most prodigious

thinkers of all time are Aquinas and Edwards. Aquinas was more prolific in his literary productions than Edwards, but, in terms of intellectual brilliance, Edwards was at least his peer, if not his superior. He was to theology what Newton and Einstein were to physics.

The value of Edwards's work is not found merely in his lucid and penetrating mind. What is most singular is his combination of rational analysis with spiritual ardor. Here was a man whose heart was aflame with love and devotion for the sweetness and excellence of Christ. His work exudes authentic religious affection. He was, above all things, a lover of God who made the seeking of His Kingdom the chief business of his life.

Edwards embodied the twin principles of the primacy of the intellect and the primacy of the heart. He exhibited the primacy of the intellect in terms of order. That is, he understood that though there can be a quasi-knowledge of God in the mind that never pierces the soul or inflames the heart, there can never be a passion of the soul that is not first awakened in the understanding. Edwards's pursuit of the knowledge of God was never an end in itself. It always served a higher purpose: to move the soul to adoration and the heart to obedient faith.

For Edwards, the primacy of the heart was a primacy of *importance*. Though the heart follows the mind in the temporal order of learning, the most important dimension of genuine faith was the response of the heart to God. The things of God captured Edwards's heart and invested it with an all-consuming passion of love.

When teaching my course on the sermons of Edwards, I introduce it with a bold claim. I assert that, "In all probability this will be the most significant and life-changing course you will ever take." I hasten to add, "The significance of this course will have nothing to do with the one who teaches it, but will rest in the exposure you have to Edwards." The student who discovers the treasures contained in the writings of Edwards is a student whose life will be unalterably changed. Edwards takes us to a new level of understanding and sets a new standard of godliness that wreaks havoc upon the level we were previously satisfied with. In this respect, the reading of Edwards is a dangerous business. But it is a delightful business worth all the peril it involves. What we risk is simply the loss of the enticements of the world, the flesh, and the devil.

Soli Deo Gloria has provided a marvelous service to the church by re-issuing these sermons of Edwards in an updated version of punctuation and style that enhances the readability of Edwards's writings for the contemporary reader. It will bring us face to face with the One who is "Altogether Lovely."

R. C. Sproul
Orlando
September, 1997

God the Best Portion of the Christian

"Whom have I in heaven but Thee? and there is none upon earth that I desire besides Thee." Psalm 73:25

In this psalm, the psalmist (Asaph) relates the great difficulty which existed in his own mind from the consideration of the wicked. He observes in verses 2 and 3: "As for me, my feet were almost gone; my steps had well nigh slipped. For I was envious at the foolish, when I saw the prosperity of the wicked." In the 4th and following verses he informs us what in the wicked was his temptation. In the first place, he observed that they were prosperous and all things went well with them. He then observed their behavior in their prosperity, and the use which they made of it, and that God, notwithstanding such abuse, continued their prosperity. Then he tells us by what means he was helped out of this difficulty: by going into the sanctuary (verses 16–17), and proceeds to inform us what considerations they were which helped him:

The consideration of the miserable end of the wicked men. However they prosper for the present, yet they come to a woeful end at last (verses 18–20).

The consideration of the blessed end of the saints. Although the saints, while they live, may be afflicted, yet they come to a happy end at last (verses 21–24).

The consideration that the godly have a much better portion than the wicked, even though they have no other portion but God (verses 25–26). Though the wicked are in prosperity, and are not in trouble as other men, yet the godly, though in affliction, are in a state infinitely better because they have God for their portion. They need desire nothing else. He who has God has all. Thus the psalmist professes the sense and apprehension which he had of things: "Whom have I in heaven but Thee? and there is none upon earth that I desire besides Thee."

In the verse immediately preceding, the psalmist takes notice how the saints are happy in God, both when they are in this world and also when they are taken to another. They are blessed in God in this world, in that He guides them by His counsel. And when He takes them out of this world they are still happy, in that then He receives them to glory. This probably led him in the text to declare that he desired no other portion, either in this world or in that to come, either in heaven or upon earth. Whence we learn that it is the spirit of a truly godly man to prefer God before all other things, either in heaven or on earth.

I. A godly man prefers God before anything else in heaven.

1. He prefers God before anything else that actually is in heaven. Every godly man has his heart in heaven; his affections are mainly set on what is to be had there. Heaven is his chosen country and inheritance. He has respect to heaven as a traveler who is in a distant land has to his own country. The traveler can content himself to be in a strange land for a while, but his own native land is preferred by him to all others. Hebrews 11:13–16: "These all died in faith, not having received the promises, but were persuaded of them, and embraced them, and confessed that they were strangers and pilgrims on the earth. For they that say such things declare plainly that they seek a country. And truly if they had been mindful of that country from whence they came out, they

might have had opportunity to have returned; but now they desire a better country, that is, a heavenly." The respect which a godly person has to heaven may be compared to the respect which a child when he is abroad has to his father's house. He can be contented abroad for a little while, but the place to which he desires to return, and in which to dwell, is his own home. Heaven is the true saint's Father's house. John 14:2: "In My Father's house are many mansions." John 20:17: "I ascend to My Father and your Father."

Now the main reason why the godly man has his heart thus to heaven is because God is there; that is the palace of the Most High. It is the place where God is gloriously present, where His love is gloriously manifested, where the godly may be with Him, see Him as He is, and love, serve, praise, and enjoy Him perfectly. If God and Christ were not in heaven, he would not be so earnest in seeking it, nor would he take so much pains in a laborious travel through this wilderness, nor would the consideration that he is going to heaven when he dies be such a comfort to him under toils and afflictions. The martyrs would not undergo cruel sufferings from their persecutors with a cheerful prospect of going to heaven did they not expect to be with Christ and to enjoy God there. They would not with that cheerfulness forsake all their earthly possessions, and all their earthly friends, as many thousands of them have done, and wander about in poverty and banishment, being destitute, afflicted, and tormented, in hopes of exchanging their earthly for a heavenly inheritance, were it not that they hope to be with their glorious Redeemer and heavenly Father. The believer's heart is in heaven because his treasure is there.

2. A godly man prefers God before anything else that might be in heaven. Not only is there nothing actually in heaven which is, in his esteem, equal with God, but neither is

there any of which he can conceive as possible to be there, which by him is esteemed and desired equally with God. Some suppose quite different enjoyments to be in heaven from those which the Scriptures teach us. The Mohammedans, for instance, suppose that in heaven are to be enjoyed all manner of sensual delights and pleasures. Many things which Mohammed has feigned are to the lusts and carnal appetites of men the most agreeable that he could devise, and with them he flattered his followers. But the true saint could not contrive one more agreeable to his inclination and desires, than such as is revealed in the Word of God—a heaven of enjoying the glorious God and the Lord Jesus Christ. There he shall have all sin taken away, and shall be perfectly conformed to God; he shall spend an eternity in exalted exercises of love to Him, and in the enjoyment of His love. If God were not to be enjoyed in heaven, but only vast wealth, immense treasures of silver and gold, great honor of such kind as men obtain in this world, and a fullness of the greatest sensual delights and pleasures—all these things would not make up for the want of God and Christ, and the enjoyment of them there. If heaven were empty of God, it would indeed be an empty, melancholy place. The godly have been made sensible, as to all creature-enjoyments, that they cannot satisfy the soul; and therefore nothing will content them but God. Offer a saint what you will, if you deny him God he will esteem himself miserable. God is the center of his desires; and as long as you keep his soul from its proper center it will not be at rest.

II. It is the temper of a godly man to prefer God before all other things on the earth.

1. The saint prefers that enjoyment of God, for which he hopes hereafter, to anything in this world. He looks not so much at the things which are seen and temporal as at those

which are unseen and eternal (2 Corinthians 4:18). It is but a little of God that the saint enjoys in this world; he has but a little acquaintance with God, and enjoys but a little of the manifestations of the divine glory and love. But God has promised to give him Himself hereafter in full enjoyment. And these promises are more precious to the saint than the most precious earthly jewels. The gospel contains greater treasures, in his esteem, than the cabinets of princes or the mines of the Indies.

2. The saints prefer what of God may be obtained in this life before all things in the world. There is a great difference in the present spiritual attainments of the saints. Some attain to much greater acquaintance and communion with God, and conformity to Him, than others. But the highest attainments are very small in comparison with what is future. The saints are capable of making progress in spiritual attainments, and they earnestly desire such further attainments. Not contented with those degrees to which they have already attained, they hunger and thirst after righteousness, and, as newborn babes, desire the sincere milk of the Word that they may grow thereby. It is their desire to know more of God, to have more of His image, and to be enabled more to imitate God and Christ in their walk and conversation. Psalm 27:4: "One thing have I desired of the Lord, that will I seek after: that I may dwell in the house of the Lord all the days of my life, to behold the beauty of the Lord, and to inquire in His temple." Psalm 42:1–2: "As the hart panteth after the water-brooks, so panteth my soul after Thee, O God. My soul thirsteth for God, for the living God: when shall I come and appear before God?" Psalm 63:1–2: "O God, Thou art my God, early will I seek Thee. My soul thirsteth for Thee, my flesh longeth for Thee in a dry and thirsty land where no water is; to see Thy power and Thy glory, so as I have seen Thee in the sanctuary."

See also Psalm 84:1–3 and Psalm 130:6: "My soul waiteth for the Lord more than they that watch for the morning; I say, more than they that watch for the morning."

Though every saint has not this longing desire after God to the same degree that the psalmist had, yet they are all of the same spirit: they earnestly desire to have more of His presence in their hearts. That this is the temper of the godly in general, and not of some particular saints only, appears from Isaiah 26:8–9 where not any particular saint, but the Church in general, speaks thus: "Yea, in the way of Thy judgments, O Lord, have we waited for Thee; the desire of our soul is to Thy name, and to the remembrance of Thee. With my soul have I desired Thee in the night, and with my spirit within me will I seek Thee early." See also Song of Solomon 3:1–2; 6–8.

The saints are not always in the lively exercise of grace; but such a spirit they have, and sometimes they have the sensible exercise of it. They desire God and divine attainments more than all earthly things, and seek to be rich in grace more than they do to get earthly riches. They desire the honor which is of God more than that which is of men (John 5:44), and communion with Him more than any earthly pleasures. They are of the same spirit which the Apostle expresses in Philippians 3:8: "Yea, doubtless, and I count all things but loss for the excellency of the knowledge of Christ Jesus, my Lord, and do count them but dung that I may win Christ."

3. The saint prefers what he has already of God before anything in this world. That which was infused into his heart at his conversion is more precious to him than anything which the world can afford. The views which are sometimes given him of the beauty and excellency of God are more precious to him than all the treasures of the wicked. The relation of a child in which he stands to God, the union which there is

between his soul and Jesus Christ, he values more than the greatest earthly dignity. That image of God which is stamped on his soul he values more than any earthly ornaments. It is, in his esteem, better to be adorned with the graces of God's Holy Spirit than to be made to shine in jewels of gold and the most costly pearls, or to be admired for the greatest external beauty. He values the robe of Christ's righteousness, which he has on his soul, more than the robes of princes. The spiritual pleasures and delights which he sometimes has in God he prefers far before all the pleasures of sin. Psalm 84:10: "A day in Thy courts is better than a thousand. I had rather be a doorkeeper in the house of God than to dwell in the tents of wickedness."

A saint thus prefers God before all other things in this world. Whatever temporal enjoyments he has, he prefers God to them all. Psalm 16:5–6: "The Lord is the portion of mine inheritance, and of my cup. Thou maintainest my lot. The lines are fallen to me in pleasant places; yea, I have a goodly heritage." If he is rich, he chiefly sets his heart on his heavenly riches. He prefers God before any earthly friend, and the divine favor before any respect shown him by his fellow creatures. Although inadvertently these have room in his heart, and too much room, yet he reserves the throne for God. Luke 14:26: "If any man come to Me, and hate not his father and mother, and wife, and children, and brethren, and sisters, yea, and his own life also, he cannot be My disciple."

He prefers God before any earthly enjoyment of which he has a prospect. The children of men commonly set their hearts more on some earthly happiness for which they hope, and after which they are seeking, than on what they have in present possession. But a godly man prefers God to anything which he has in prospect in this world. He may, indeed, through the prevalence of corruption, for a season be carried away with some enjoyment; however, he will again come to himself; this is not the temper of the man; he is of another spirit.

It is the spirit of a godly man to prefer God to any earthly enjoyments of which he can conceive. He not only prefers Him to anything which he now possesses, but he sees nothing possessed by any of his fellow creatures as so estimable. Could he have as much worldly prosperity as he would, could he have earthly things just to his mind, and agreeable to his inclination, he values the portion which he has in God incomparably more. He prefers Christ to earthly kingdoms.

Application

1. Hence we may learn that whatever changes a godly man passes through, he is happy because God, who is unchangeable, is his chosen portion. Though he meets with temporal losses, and is deprived of many, yea, of all his temporal enjoyments, yet God, whom he prefers before all, still remains and cannot be lost. While he stays in this changeable, troublesome world he is happy, because his chosen portion, on which he builds as his main foundation for happiness, is above the world, and above all changes. And when he goes into another world, still he is happy because that portion yet remains. Whatever he is deprived of, he cannot be deprived of his chief portion; his inheritance remains sure to him. Could worldly-minded men find a way to secure to themselves those earthly enjoyments on which they mainly set their hearts, so that they could not be lost nor impaired while they live, how great would they account the privilege, though other things which they esteem in a lesser degree were liable to the same uncertainty as they now are! Whereas now those earthly enjoyments on which men chiefly set their hearts are often

most fading. But how great is the happiness of those who have chosen the Fountain of all good, who prefer Him before all things in heaven or on earth, and who can never be deprived of Him to all eternity!

2. By these things, let all examine and try themselves whether they are saints or not. As this which has been exhibited is the spirit of the saints, so it is peculiar to them; none can use the language of the text and say, "Whom have I in heaven but Thee? There is none upon earth that I desire besides Thee" but the saints. A man's choice is that which determines his state. He who chooses God for his portion, and prefers Him to all other things, is a godly man, for he chooses and worships Him as God. To respect Him as God is to respect Him above all other things; and if any man respects Him as his God, his God He is. There is a union and covenant relation between that man and the true God. Every man is as his God is. If you would know what a man is, whether he is a godly man or not, you must inquire what his God is. If the true God is He to whom he has a supreme respect, whom he regards above all, he is doubtless a servant of the true God. But if the man has something else to which he pays a greater respect than to Jehovah, he is not a godly man.

Inquire, therefore, how it is with you, whether you prefer God before all other things. It may sometimes be a difficulty for persons to determine this to their satisfaction. The ungodly may be deluded with false affections; the godly in dull frames may be at a loss about it. Therefore you may try yourselves as to this matter in several ways; if you cannot speak fully to one thing, yet you may perhaps to others.

1. What is it which chiefly makes you desire to go to heaven when you die? Indeed some have no great desire to go to heaven. They do not care to go to hell, but if they could be safe from that they would not much concern themselves

about heaven. If it is not so with you, but you find that you have a desire after heaven, then inquire what it is for. Is the main reason that you may be with God, have communion with Him, and be conformed to Him? that you may see God and enjoy Him there? Is this the consideration which keeps your hearts, your desires, and your expectations towards heaven?

2. If you could avoid death and might have your free choice, would you choose to live always in this world without God rather than in His time to leave the world in order to be with Him? If you might live here in earthly prosperity to all eternity, but destitute of the presence of God and communion with Him—having no spiritual intercourse between Him and your souls, God and you being strangers to each other forever—would you choose this rather than to leave the world in order to dwell in heaven as the children of God, there to enjoy the glorious privileges of children in a holy and perfect love to God, and enjoyment of Him to all eternity?

3. Do you prefer Christ to all others as the way to heaven? He who truly chooses God, prefers Him in each person of the Trinity, Father, Son, and Holy Ghost: the Father as his Father, the Son as his Savior, and the Holy Ghost as his Sanctifier. Inquire, therefore, not only whether you choose the enjoyment of God in heaven as your highest portion and happiness, but also whether you choose Jesus Christ before all others as your way to heaven—and that in a sense of the excellency of Christ and of the way of salvation by Him as being that which is to the glory of Christ and of sovereign grace. Is the way of free grace, by the blood and righteousness of the blessed and glorious Redeemer, the most excellent way to life in your esteem? Does it add a value to the heavenly inheritance that it is conferred in this way? Is this far better to you than to be saved by your own righteousness, by any of your performances, or by any other mediator?

4. If you might go to heaven in what course you please, would you prefer to all others the way of a strict walk with God? They who prefer God as has been represented choose Him not only in the end, but in the way. They would rather be with God than with any other, not only when they come to the end of their journey, but also while they are in their pilgrimage. They choose the way of walking with God, though it is a way of labor, care, and self-denial rather than a way of sin, though it is a way of sloth and of gratifying their lusts.

5. Were you to spend your eternity in this world, would you choose rather to live in mean and low circumstances with the gracious presence of God than to live forever in earthly prosperity without Him? Would you rather spend it in holy living, and serving and walking with God, and in the enjoyment of the privileges of His children? God often manifests Himself to you as your Father, reveals to you His glory, manifests His love, and lifts the light of His countenance upon you! Would you rather choose these things, though in poverty, than to abound in worldly things, and to live in ease and prosperity, at the same time being an alien from the commonwealth of Israel? Could you be content to stand in no childlike relation to God, enjoying no gracious intercourse with Him, having no right to be acknowledged by Him as His children? Or would such a life as this, though in ever so great earthly prosperity, be esteemed by you as a miserable life?

If, after all, there remain with you doubts, and a difficulty to determine concerning yourselves whether you do truly and sincerely prefer God to all other things, I would mention two things which are the surest ways to be determined in this matter, and which seem to be the best grounds of satisfaction in it.

First, the feeling of some particular, strong, and lively exercise of such a spirit. A person may have such a spirit as is spoken of in the doctrine, and may have the exercise of it in a low degree, and yet remain in doubt whether he has it or not and be unable to come to a satisfying determination. But God is pleased sometimes to give such discoveries of His glory and of the excellency of Christ as so draw forth the heart that they know beyond all doubt that they feel such a spirit as Paul spoke of when he said that he counted all things but loss for the excellency of Christ Jesus his Lord; and they can boldly say, as in the text, "Whom have I in heaven but Thee? and there is none upon earth that I desire besides Thee." At such times the people of God do not need any help of ministers to satisfy them whether they have the true love of God; they plainly see and feel it, and the Spirit of God then witnesses with their spirits that they are the children of God. Therefore, if you would be satisfied upon this point, earnestly seek such attainments; seek that you may have such clear and lively exercises of this spirit. To this end, you must labor to grow in grace. Though you have had such experiences in times past, and they satisfied you then, yet you may again doubt. You should therefore seek that you may have them more frequently. And the way to that is earnestly to press forward that you may have more acquaintance with God, and have the principles of grace strengthened. This is the way to have the exercises of grace stronger, more lively, and more frequent, and so to be satisfied that you have a spirit of supreme love to God.

Second, the other way is to inquire whether you prefer God to all other things in practice, i.e., when you have occasion to manifest by your practice which you prefer—when you must either cleave to one or the other, and must either forsake other things, or forsake God—whether then it is your manner practically to prefer God to all other things whatsoever, even to those earthly things to which your hearts are most wedded. Are your lives those of adherence to God, and of serving Him in this manner?

He who sincerely prefers God to all other things in his heart will do it in his practice. For when God and all other things come to stand in competition, that is the proper trial, what a man chooses; and the manner of acting in such cases must certainly determine what the choice is in all free agents, or those who act on choice. Therefore there is no sign of sincerity so much insisted on in the Bible as this: that we deny ourselves, sell all, forsake the world, take up the cross, and follow Christ whithersoever He goes. Therefore, so run, not as uncertainly; so fight, not as those that beat the air; but keep under your bodies and bring them into subjection. Act not as though you counted yourselves to have apprehended, but this one thing do: "forgetting those things which are behind, and reaching forth unto those things which are before, press toward the mark, for the prize of the high calling of God in Christ Jesus" (Philippians 3:13–14)). "And besides this, giving diligence, add to your faith, virtue; and to virtue, knowledge; and to knowledge, temperance; and to temperance, patience; and to patience, godliness; and to godliness, brotherly kindness; and to brotherly kindness, charity. For if these things be in you, and abound, they make you that ye shall neither be barren nor unfruitful in the knowledge of our Lord Jesus Christ" (2 Peter 1:5–8).

The Excellency of Christ

"And one of the elders saith unto me, 'Weep not: Behold, the Lion of the tribe of Judah, the Root of David, hath prevailed to open the book, and to loose the seven seals thereof.' And I beheld, and, lo, in the midst of the throne and of the four beasts, and in the midst of the elders, stood a Lamb as it had been slain." Revelation 5:5–6

    The visions and revelations the apostle John had of the future events of God's providence are here introduced with a vision of the book of God's decrees, by which those events were foreordained. This is represented (verse 1) as a book in the right hand of Him who sat on the throne, "written within and on the back side, and sealed with seven seals." Books, in the form in which they were wont of old to be made, were broad leaves of parchment of paper, or something of that nature, joined together at one edge, and so rolled up together, and then sealed or in some way fastened together, to prevent their unfolding and opening. Hence we read of the scroll of a book (Jeremiah 36:2). It seems to have been such a book that John had a vision of here; and therefore it is said to be "written within and on the back side," i.e., on the inside pages, and also on one of the outside pages—that which was rolled in rolling the book up together. And it is said to be "sealed with seven seals," to signify that what was written in it was perfectly hidden and secret; or that God's decrees of future events are sealed, and shut up from all possibility of being discovered by creatures till God is pleased to make them known. We find that seven is often used in Scripture as the number of perfection, to signify the superlative or most perfect degree of any thing; which probably arose from this: that on the seventh day God beheld the works of creation finished and rested and rejoiced in them as being complete and perfect.

When John saw this book, he tells us that he "saw a strong angel proclaiming with a loud voice, 'Who is worthy to open the book, and to loose the seals thereof?' And no man in heaven, nor in earth, neither under the earth, was able to open the book, neither to look thereon." And he wept much because "no man was found worthy to open and read the book, neither to look thereon." And then he tells us how his tears were dried up, in that "one of the elders said unto him, 'Weep not; Behold the Lion of the tribe of Judah hath prevailed,' " as in our text. Though no man, nor angel, nor any mere creature was found either able to loose the seals or worthy to be admitted to the privilege of reading the book, yet this was declared for the comfort of this beloved disciple, that Christ was found both able and worthy. And we have an account in the succeeding chapters how He actually did it, opening the seals in order, first one, and then another, revealing what God had decreed should come to pass hereafter. And we have an account in this chapter of His coming and taking the book out of the right hand of Him who sat on the throne, and of the joyful praises that were sung to Him in heaven and earth on that occasion.

Many things might be observed in the words of the text; but it is to my present purpose only to take notice of the two distinct appellations here given to Christ:

1. He is called a Lion. "Behold, the Lion of the tribe of Judah." He seems to be called the Lion of the tribe of Judah in allusion to what Jacob said in his blessing of the tribes on his deathbed, who, when he came to bless Judah, compared him to a lion. Genesis 49:9: "Judah is a lion's whelp; from the prey, my son, thou art gone up: he stooped down, he couched

as a lion, and as an old lion; who shall rouse him up?" And it also alludes to the standard of the camp of Judah in the wilderness on which was displayed a lion, according to the ancient tradition of the Jews. It is much on account of the valiant acts of David that the tribe of Judah, of which David was, is in Jacob's prophetic blessing compared to a lion; but more especially with an eye to Jesus Christ, who also was of that tribe, and was descended of David, and is in our text called "the Root of David." Therefore Christ is here called "the Lion of the tribe of Judah."

2. He is called a Lamb. John was told of a Lion that had prevailed to open the book, and probably expected to see a lion in his vision; but while he is expecting, behold, a Lamb appears to open the book, an exceedingly diverse kind of creature from a lion. A lion is a devourer, one that is wont to make terrible slaughter of others; and no creature more easily falls a prey to him than a lamb. And Christ is here represented not only as a Lamb, a creature very liable to be slain, but a "Lamb as it had been slain," that is, with the marks of its deadly wounds appearing on it.

That which I would observe from the words for the subject of my present discourse is this: There is an admirable conjunction of diverse excellencies in Jesus Christ.

The lion and the lamb, though very diverse kinds of creatures, yet have each their peculiar excellencies. The lion excels in strength, and in the majesty of his appearance and voice. The lamb excels in meekness and patience, besides the excellent nature of the creature as good for food, and yielding that which is fit for our clothing and being suitable to be offered in sacrifice to God. But we see that Christ is, in the text, compared to both, because the diverse excellencies of both wonderfully meet in Him.

In handling this subject I would, first, show wherein there

is an admirable conjunction of diverse excellencies in Christ; second, show how this admirable conjunction of excellencies appears in Christ's acts; and then make application.

First, I would show wherein there is an admirable conjunction of diverse excellencies in Jesus Christ, which appears in three things:

I. There is a conjunction of such excellencies in Christ as, in our manner of conceiving, are very diverse one from another.

II. There is in Him a conjunction of such really diverse excellencies as otherwise would have seemed to us utterly incompatible in the same object.

III. Such diverse excellencies are exercised in Him towards men who otherwise would have seemed impossible to be exercised towards the same object.

I. There is a conjunction of such excellencies in Christ as, in our manner of conceiving, are very diverse one from another. Such are the various divine perfections and excellencies of which Christ is possessed. Christ is a divine person, and therefore has all the attributes of God. The difference between these is chiefly relative, and in our manner of conceiving them. And those which, in this sense, are most diverse meet in the person of Christ. I shall mention two instances.

1. There meet in Jesus Christ infinite highness and infinite condescension. Christ, as He is God, is infinitely great and high above all. He is higher than the kings of the earth for He is King of kings and Lord of lords. He is higher than the heavens, and higher than the highest angels of heaven. So great is He that all men, all kings and princes, are as worms of the dust before Him; all nations are as the drop of the bucket, and the light dust of the balance; yea, and angels themselves are as nothing before Him. He is so high that He is infinitely

above any need of us, so above our conceptions that we cannot comprehend Him. Proverbs 30:4: "What is His name, and what is His Son's name, if thou canst tell?" Our understandings, if we stretch them never so far, cannot reach up to His divine glory. Job 11:8: "It is high as heaven, what canst thou do?" Christ is the Creator and great Possessor of heaven and earth. He is sovereign Lord of all. He rules over the whole universe and does whatsoever pleases Him. His knowledge is without bound. His wisdom is perfect, and what none can circumvent. His power is infinite and none can resist Him. His riches are immense and inexhaustible. His majesty is infinitely awful.

And yet He is one of infinite condescension. None are so low or inferior but Christ's condescension is sufficient to take a gracious notice of them. He condescends not only to the angels, humbling Himself to behold the things that are done in heaven, but He also condescends to such poor creatures as men; and that not only so as to take notice of princes and great men, but of those who are of meanest rank and degree, "the poor of the world" (James 2:5). Such as are commonly despised by their fellow creatures, Christ does not despise. 1 Corinthians 1:28: "Base things of the world, and things that are despised, hath God chosen." Christ condescends to take notice of beggars (Luke 16:22) and people of the most despised nations. In Christ Jesus there is neither "barbarian, Scythian, bond nor free" (Colossians 3:11). He who is so high condescends to take a gracious notice of little children. Matthew 19:14: "Suffer the little children to come unto Me." Yea, which is more, His condescension is sufficient to take a gracious notice of the most unworthy, sinful creatures, those who have no good deservings and those who have infinite ill deservings.

Yea, so great is His condescension that it is not only sufficient to take some gracious notice of such as these, but sufficient for everything that is an act of condescension. His condescension is great enough to become their friend, to become their companion, to unite their souls to Him in spiritual marriage. It is enough to take their nature upon Him, to become one *of* them that He may be one *with* them. Yea, it is great enough to abase Himself yet lower for them, even to expose Himself to shame and spitting; yea, to yield up Himself to an ignominious death for them. And what greater act of condescension can be conceived? Yet such an act as this has His condescension yielded to, for those who are so low and mean, despicable and unworthy!

Such a conjunction of infinite highness and low condescension in the same person is admirable. We see by manifold instances what a tendency a high station has in men to make them to be of a quite contrary disposition. If one worm is a little exalted above another by having more dust or a bigger dunghill, how much does he make of himself! What a distance does he keep from those that are below him! And a little condescension is what he expects should be made much of and greatly acknowledged. Christ condescends to wash our feet; but how would great men (or rather bigger worms) account themselves debased by acts of far less condescension!

2. There meet in Jesus Christ infinite justice and infinite grace. As Christ is a divine person, He is infinitely holy and just, hating sin, and disposed to execute condign punishment for sin. He is the Judge of the world, and the infinitely just Judge of it, and will not at all acquit the wicked or by any means clear the guilty.

And yet He is infinitely gracious and merciful. Though His justice is so strict, with respect to all sin and every branch of the law, yet He has grace sufficient for every sinner, and even the chief of sinners. And it is not only sufficient to show mercy to the most unworthy and bestow some good upon them, but to bestow the greatest good; yea, it is sufficient to bestow all good upon them, and to do all things for them. There is no benefit or blessing that they can receive so great but the grace of Christ is sufficient to bestow it on the greatest sinner that ever lived. And not only so, but so great is His grace that nothing is too much as the means of this good. It is sufficient not only to do great things, but also to suffer in order to achieve it; and not only to suffer, but to suffer most extremely even unto death, the most ignominious and tormenting and in every way the most terrible that men could inflict; yea, and greater sufferings than men could inflict who could only torment the body. He had sufferings in His soul that were the more immediate fruits of the wrath of God against the sins of those He undertakes for.

II. There meet in the person of Christ such really diverse excellencies, which otherwise would have been incompatible in the same subject; such as are conjoined in no other person whatsoever, either divine, human, or angelic; and such as neither men nor angels would ever have imagined could have met together in the same person, had it not been seen in the person of Christ. I would give some instances.

1. In the person of Christ meet together infinite glory and lowest humility. Infinite glory and the virtue of humility meet in no other person but Christ. They meet in no created person, for no created person has infinite glory; and they meet in no other divine person but Christ. For though the divine nature is infinitely abhorrent to pride, yet humility is not properly attributable to God the Father and the Holy Ghost, who exist only in the divine nature; because it is proper excellency only of a created nature, for it consists radically in a sense of a comparative lowness and littleness before God, or the great

distance between God and the subject of this virtue. But it would be a contradiction to suppose any such thing in God.

But in Jesus Christ, who is both God and man, those two diverse excellencies are sweetly united. He is a person infinitely exalted in glory and dignity. Philippians 2:6: "Being in the form of God, He thought it not robbery to be equal with God." There is equal honor due to Him with the Father. John 5:23: "That all men should honor the Son, even as they honor the Father." God Himself says to Him, "Thy throne, O God, is forever and ever" (Hebrews 1:8). And there is the same supreme respect and divine worship paid to Him by the angels of heaven as to God the Father in verse 6: "Let all the angels of God worship Him."

But however He is thus above all, yet He is lowest of all in humility. There never was so great an instance of this virtue among either men or angels as Jesus. None ever was so sensible of the distance between Himself and God as the man Christ Jesus (Matthew 11:29). What a wonderful spirit of humility appeared in Him when He was here upon earth in all His behavior! In His contentment, in His mean outward condition, contentedly living in the family of Joseph the carpenter and Mary His mother for thirty years together, and afterwards choosing outward meanness, poverty, and contempt rather than earthly greatness; in His washing His disciples' feet, and in all His speeches and deportment towards them; in His cheerfully sustaining the form of a servant through His whole life, and submitting to such immense humiliation at death!

2. In the person of Christ meet together infinite majesty and transcendent meekness. These again are two qualifications that meet together in no other person but Christ. Meekness, properly so called, is a virtue proper only to the creature; we scarcely ever find meekness mentioned as a di-

vine attribute in Scripture, at least not in the New Testament; for thereby seems to be signified a calmness and quietness of spirit arising from humility in mutable beings who are naturally liable to be put into a world. But Christ, being both God and man, has both infinite majesty and superlative meekness.

Christ was a person of infinite majesty. It is He who is spoken of in Psalm 45:3: "Gird Thy sword upon Thy thigh, O Most Mighty, with Thy glory and Thy majesty." It is He who is mighty, who rides on the heavens and His excellency on the sky. It is He who is terrible out of His holy places; who is mightier than the noise of many waters, yea, than the mighty waves of the sea; before whom a fire goes and burns up His enemies round about; at whose presence the earth quakes and the hills melt; who sits on the circle of the earth, and all the inhabitants thereof are as grasshoppers; who rebukes the sea, and makes it dry, and dries up the rivers; whose eyes are as a flame of fire; from whose presence, and from the glory of whose power, the wicked shall be punished with everlasting destruction; who is the blessed and only Potentate, the King of kings, and Lord of lords, who has heaven for His throne and the earth for His footstool, and is the high and lofty One who inhabits eternity; whose kingdom is an everlasting kingdom, and of whose dominion there is no end.

And yet He was the most marvelous instance of meekness and humble quietness of spirit who ever was, agreeable to the prophecies of Him in Matthew 21:4–5: "All this was done, that it might be fulfilled which was spoken by the prophet, saying, 'Tell ye the daughter of Zion, "Behold, thy King cometh unto thee, meek, and sitting upon an ass, and a colt the foal of an ass." ' " And it is agreeable to what Christ declares of Himself in Matthew 11:29: "I am meek and lowly in heart." And it is agreeable to what was manifest in His behavior, for there never was such an instance seen on earth of a meek behavior

The Excellency of Christ

under injuries and reproaches, and towards enemies; who, when He was reviled, reviled not again. He had a wonderful spirit of forgiveness, was ready to forgive His worst enemies, and prayed for them with fervent and effectual prayers. With what meekness did He appear in the ring of soldiers who were condemning and mocking Him. He was silent and opened not His mouth, but went as a lamb to the slaughter. Thus is Christ—a Lion in majesty and a Lamb in meekness.

3. There meet in the person of Christ the deepest reverence towards God and equality with God. Christ, when on earth, appeared full of holy reverence towards the Father. He paid the most reverential worship to Him, praying to Him with postures of reverence. Thus we read of His "kneeling down and praying" (Luke 22:41). This became Christ, as one who had taken on Himself the human nature; but at the same time He existed in the divine nature, whereby His person was in all respects equal to the person of the Father. God the Father has no attribute or perfection that the Son has not in equal degree and equal glory. These things meet in no other person but Jesus Christ.

4. There are conjoined in the person of Christ infinite worthiness of good and the greatest patience under sufferings of evil. He was perfectly innocent and deserved no suffering. He deserved nothing from God by any guilt of His own; and He deserved no ill from men. Yea, He was not only harmless and undeserving of suffering, but He was infinitely worthy: worthy of the infinite love of the Father, worthy of infinite and eternal happiness, and infinitely worthy of all possible esteem, love, and service from all men. And yet He was perfectly patient under the greatest sufferings that ever were endured in this world. Hebrews 12:2: "He endured the cross, despising the shame." He suffered not from His Father for His faults, but ours; and He suffered from men not for His faults, but for

those things on account of which He was infinitely worthy of their love and honor; which made His patience the more wonderful and the more glorious. 1 Peter 2:20–24: "For what glory is it, if, when ye be buffeted for your faults, ye shall take it patiently? But if when ye do well, and suffer for it, ye take it patiently, this is acceptable with God. For even hereunto were ye called; because Christ also suffered for us, leaving us an example, that we should follow His steps: who did no sin, neither was guile found in His mouth; who, when He was reviled, reviled not again; when He suffered, He threatened not, but committed Himself to Him that judgeth righteously: who His own self bare our sins in His own body on the tree, that we, being dead to sin, should live unto righteousness; by whose stripes ye were healed." There is no such conjunction of innocence, worthiness, and patience under sufferings as in the person of Christ.

5. In the person of Christ are conjoined an exceeding spirit of obedience with supreme dominion over heaven and earth. Christ is the Lord of all things in two respects. First, He is so as God-man and Mediator; and thus His dominion is appointed and given Him by the Father. Having it by delegation from God, He is, as it were, the Father's vice-regent. But, second, He is Lord of all things in another respect: as He is (by His original nature) God, and so He is by natural right the Lord of all, and supreme over all as much as the Father. Thus, He has dominion over the world not by delegation, but in His own right. He is not an "under-god," as the Arians suppose, but, to all intents and purposes, supreme God.

And yet in the same person is found the greatest spirit of obedience to the commands and laws of God that ever was in the universe; which was manifest in His obedience here in this world. John 14:31: "As the Father gave Me commandment, even so I do." John 15:10: "Even as I have kept My Father's commandments, and abide in His love." The greatness of His obedience appears in its perfection, and in His obeying commands of such exceeding difficulty. Never did anyone receive commands from God of such difficulty, and that were so great a trial of obedience, as Jesus Christ. One of God's commands to Him was that He should yield Himself to those dreadful sufferings that He underwent. See John 10:18: "No man taketh it from Me, but I lay it down of Myself. This commandment received I of My Father." And Christ was thoroughly obedient to this command of God. Hebrews 5:8: "Though He were a Son, yet He learned obedience by the things that He suffered." Philippians 2:8: "He humbled Himself, and became obedient unto death, even the death of the cross." Never was there such an instance of obedience in man or angel as this, though He was at the same time supreme Lord of both angels and men.

6. In the person of Christ are conjoined absolute sovereignty and perfect resignation. This is another unparalleled conjunction. Christ, as He is God, is the absolute sovereign of the world, the sovereign disposer of all events. The decrees of God are all His sovereign decrees; and the work of creation, and all God's works of providence, are His sovereign works. It is He who works all things according to the counsel of His own will. Colossians 1:16–17: "By Him, and through Him, and to Him, are all things." John 5:17: "The Father worketh hitherto, and I work." Matthew 8:3: "I will, be thou clean."

But yet Christ was the most wonderful instance of resignation that ever appeared in the world. He was absolutely and perfectly resigned when He had a near and immediate prospect of His terrible sufferings and the dreadful cup that He was to drink. The idea and expectation of this made His soul exceedingly sorrowful, even unto death, and put Him into such an agony that His sweat was, as it were, great drops of blood clotting down to the ground. But in such circumstances He was wholly resigned to the will of God. Matthew 26:39: "O My Father, if it be possible, let this cup pass from Me; nevertheless, not as I will, but as Thou wilt." Verse 42: "O My Father, if this cup may not pass from Me, except I drink it, Thy will be done."

7. In Christ meet together self-sufficiency and an entire trust and reliance on God; which is another conjunction peculiar to the person of Christ. As He is a divine person, He is self-sufficient, standing in need of nothing. All creatures are dependent on Him, but He is dependent on none, but is absolutely independent. His proceeding from the Father in His eternal generation of filiation argues no proper dependence on the will of the Father; for that proceeding was natural and necessary, and not arbitrary. But yet Christ entirely trusted in God. His enemies say that of Him: "He trusted in God that He would deliver Him" (Matthew 27:43). And the Apostle testifies in 1 Peter 2:23 that "He committed Himself to God."

III. Such diverse excellencies are expressed in Him towards men who otherwise would have seemed impossible to be exercised towards the same object; as particularly these three: justice, mercy, and truth. The same are mentioned in Psalm 85:10: "Mercy and truth are met together, righteousness and peace have kissed each other." The strict justice of God, and even His avenging justice, and that against the sins of men, never was so gloriously manifested as in Christ. He manifested an infinite regard to the attribute of God's justice in that, when He had a mind to save sinners, He was willing to undergo such extreme sufferings rather than that their salvation should be to the injury of the honor of that attribute. And as He is the Judge of the world, He Himself exercises strict justice. He will not clear the guilty, nor at all acquit the wicked in judgment. Yet how wonderfully is infinite mercy towards sinners displayed in Him! And what glorious and ineffable grace and love have been and are exercised by Him towards sinful men! Though He is the just Judge of a sinful world, yet He is also the Savior of the world. Though He is a consuming fire to sin, yet He is the light and life of sinners. Romans 3:25–26: "Whom God hath set forth to be a propitiation, through faith in His blood, to declare His righteousness for the remission of sins that are past, through the forbearance of God; to declare, I say, at this time His righteousness, that He might be just, and the justifier of him which believeth in Jesus."

So the immutable truth of God, in the threatenings of His law against the sins of men, was never so manifested as it is in Jesus Christ; for there never was any other trial so great of the unalterableness of the truth of God in those threatenings as when sin came to be imputed to His own Son. And then in Christ has been seen already an actual complete accomplishment of those threatenings which never has been nor will be seen in any other instance; because the eternity that will be taken up in fulfilling those threatenings on others never will be finished. Christ manifested an infinite regard to this truth of God in His sufferings. And, in His judging the world, He makes the covenant of works that contains those dreadful threatenings His rule of judgment. He will see to it that it is not infringed in the least jot or tittle. He will do nothing contrary to the threatenings of the law and their complete fulfillment. And yet in Him we have many great and precious promises, promises of perfect deliverance from the penalty of the law. And this is the promise that He has promised us, even eternal life. And in Him are all the promises of God "yea, and amen."

Having thus shown wherein there is an admirable conjunction of excellencies in Jesus Christ, I now proceed, second, to show how this admirable conjunction of excellencies appears in Christ's acts.

1. It appears in what Christ did in taking on Himself our nature. In this act, His infinite condescension wonderfully appeared: that He who was God should become man; that the Word should be made flesh, and should take on Himself a nature infinitely below His original nature! And it appears yet more remarkably in the low circumstances of His incarnation: He was conceived in the womb of a poor young woman whose poverty appeared in that when she came to offer sacrifices of her purification, she brought what was allowed by the law only in case of poverty. Luke 2:24: "According to what is said in the law of the Lord, 'a pair of turtle-doves, or two young pigeons.' " This was allowed only in case the person was so poor that she was not able to offer a lamb (Leviticus 12:8).

And though His infinite condescension thus appeared in the manner of His incarnation, yet His divine dignity also appeared in it; for though He was conceived in the womb of a poor virgin, yet He was conceived there by the power of the Holy Ghost. And His divine dignity also appeared in the holiness of His conception and birth. Though He was conceived in the womb of one of the corrupt race of mankind, yet He was conceived and born without sin. The angel said to the blessed Virgin in Luke 1:35: "The Holy Ghost shall come upon thee, and the power of the Highest shall overshadow thee; therefore also that holy thing which shall be born of thee shall be called the Son of God."

His infinite condescension marvelously appeared in the manner of His birth. He was brought forth in a stable because there was no room for them in the inn. The inn was taken up by others who were looked upon as persons of greater account. The blessed Virgin, being poor and despised, was turned or shut out. Though she was in such necessitous circumstances, yet those who counted themselves her betters would not give place to her. And, therefore, in the time of her travail, she was forced to betake herself to a stable; and when the child was born it was wrapped in swaddling clothes and laid in a manger. There Christ lay a little infant; and there He eminently appeared as a lamb. But yet this feeble infant, born thus in a stable and laid in a manger, was born to conquer and triumph over Satan, that roaring lion. He came to subdue the mighty powers of darkness, and make a show of them openly, and so to restore peace on earth, manifest God's good will towards men, and bring glory to God in the highest; according as the end of His birth was declared by the joyful songs of the glorious hosts of angels appearing to the shepherds at the same time that the infant lay in the manger; whereby His divine dignity was manifested.

2. This admirable conjunction of excellencies appears in the acts and various passages of Christ's life. Though Christ dwelt in mean outward circumstances, whereby His condescension and humility especially appeared and His majesty was veiled, yet His divine dignity and glory did in many of His acts shine through the veil, and it illustriously appeared that He was not only the Son of man, but the great God.

Thus, in the circumstances of His infancy, His outward meanness appeared; yet there was something then to show forth His divine dignity in the wise men's being stirred up to come from the east to give honor to Him, their being led by a miraculous star, and coming and falling down and worshipping Him, and presenting Him with gold, frankincense, and myrrh. His humility and meekness wonderfully appeared in His subjection to His mother and reputed father when He was a child. Herein He appeared as a lamb. But His divine glory broke forth and shone when, at twelve years old, He disputed with doctors in the temple. In that He appeared, in some measure, as the Lion of the tribe of Judah.

And so, after He entered on His public ministry, His marvelous humility and meekness was manifested in His choosing to appear in such mean outward circumstances; and in being contented in them when He was so poor that He had nowhere to lay His head, and depended on the charity of some of His followers for His subsistence, as appears by the beginning of Luke 8. How meek, condescending, and familiar was His treatment of His disciples; His discourses with them, treating them as a father does His children, yea, as friends and companions. How patient, bearing such affliction and reproach, and so many injuries from the scribes and Pharisees, and others. In these things He appeared as a Lamb. And yet He, at the same time, did in many ways show forth His divine majesty and glory, particularly in the miracles He wrought, which were evidently divine works, and manifested omnipotent power, and so declared Him to be the Lion of the tribe of Judah.

His wonderful and miraculous works plainly showed Him to be the God of nature in that it appeared by them that He had all nature in His hands, and could lay an arrest upon it, and stop and change its course as He pleased. In healing the sick, opening the eyes of the blind, unstopping the ears of the deaf, and healing the lame, He showed that He was the God who framed the eye, created the ear, and was the author of the frame of man's body. By the dead's rising at His command, it appeared that He was the author and fountain of life, and that He was God the Lord, to whom belong the issues from death. By His walking on the sea in a storm, when the waves were raised, He showed Himself to be that God spoken of in Job 9:8, that treadeth "on the waves of the sea."

By His stilling the storm and calming the rage of the sea by His powerful command, saying, "Peace, be still," He showed that He has the command of the universe, and that He is that God who brings things to pass by the word of His power; who speaks and it is done, who commands and it stands fast. Psalm 65:7: "Who stilleth the noise of the seas, the noise of their waves." And Psalm 107:29: "He maketh the storm a calm, so that the waves thereof are still." And Psalm 89:8–9: "O Lord God of hosts, who is a strong Lord like unto Thee, or to Thy faithfulness round about Thee? Thou rulest the raging of the sea; when the waves thereof arise, Thou stillest them."

Christ, by casting out devils, remarkably appeared as the Lion of the tribe of Judah, and showed that He was stronger than the roaring lion that seeks whom he may devour. He commanded them to come out, and they were forced to obey. They were terribly afraid of Him; they fell down before Him and beseeched Him not to torment them. He forced a whole legion of them to forsake their hold by His powerful word; and they could not so much as enter into the swine without His permission. He showed the glory of His omniscience by telling the thoughts of men, as we have often an account. Herein He appeared to be that God spoken of in Amos 4:13: "That declareth unto man what is his thought." Thus, in the midst of His meanness and humiliation, His divine glory appeared in His miracles. John 2:11: "This beginning of miracles did Jesus in Cana of Galilee, and manifested forth His glory."

And though Christ ordinarily appeared without outward glory, and in great obscurity, yet at a certain time He threw off the veil and appeared in His divine majesty, so far as it could be outwardly manifested to men in this frail state, when He was transfigured in the mount. The apostle Peter (2 Peter 1:16–18) was an "eyewitness of His majesty, when He received from God the Father honor and glory, when there came such a voice to Him from the excellent glory, 'This is My beloved Son, in whom I am well pleased'; which voice that came from heaven we heard, when we were with Him in the holy mount."

And at the same time that Christ was wont to appear in such meekness, condescension, and humility in His familiar discourses with His disciples, appearing therein as the Lamb of God, He was also wont to appear as The Lion of the tribe of Judah, with divine authority and majesty, in His so sharply rebuking the scribes and Pharisees, and other hypocrites.

3. This admirable conjunction of excellencies remarkably appears in His offering up Himself as a sacrifice for sinners in His last sufferings. As this was the greatest thing in all the works of redemption, the greatest act of Christ in that work, so in this act especially does there appear that admirable conjunction of excellencies that has been spoken of. Christ never so much appeared as a lamb as when He was slain. "He came like a lamb to the slaughter" (Isaiah 53:7). Then He was offered up to God as a lamb without blemish and without spot; then especially did He appear to be the antitype of the lamb of the passover. 1 Corinthians 5:7: "Christ our Passover sacrificed for us." And yet in that act He did, in a special manner, appear as the Lion of the tribe of Judah—yea, in this above all other acts, in many respects, as may appear in the following things:

(1) Then was Christ in the greatest degree of His humiliation, and yet by that, above all other things, His divine glory appears. Christ's humiliation was great in being born in such a low condition, of a poor virgin and in a stable. His humiliation was great in being subject to Joseph the carpenter and Mary His mother, and afterwards living in poverty so as to have nowhere to lay His head; in suffering such manifold and bitter reproaches as He suffered while He went about preaching and working miracles. But His humiliation was never so

great as it was in His last sufferings, beginning with His agony in the garden till He expired on the cross. Never was He subject to such ignominy as then; never did He suffer so much pain in His body or such sorrow in His soul; never was He in so great an exercise of His condescension, humility, meekness, and patience as He was in these last sufferings; never was His divine glory and majesty covered with so thick and dark a veil; never did He so empty Himself and make Himself of no reputation as at this time. And yet never was His divine glory so manifested by any act of His as in yielding Himself up to these sufferings. When the fruit of it came to appear, and the mystery and ends of it came to be unfolded in its issue, then did the glory of it appear; then did it appear as the most glorious act of Christ that ever He exercised towards the creature. This act of His is celebrated by the angels and hosts of heaven with peculiar praises, as that which is above all others glorious, as you may see in the context (Revelation 5:9–12): "And they sung a new song, saying, 'Thou art worthy to take the book, and to open the seals thereof: for Thou wast slain, and hast redeemed us to God by Thy blood, out of every kindred, and tongue, and people, and nation, and hast made us unto our God kings and priests; and we shall reign on the earth.' And I beheld, and I heard the voice of many angels round about the throne, and the beasts, and the elders; and the number of them was ten thousand times ten thousand, and thousands of thousands, saying with a loud voice, 'Worthy is the Lamb that was slain to receive power, and riches, and wisdom, and strength, and honor, and glory, and blessing.' "

(2) He never in any act gave so great a manifestation of love to God, and yet never so manifested His love to those who were enemies to God, as in that act. Christ never did anything whereby His love to the Father was so eminently manifested as in His laying down His life under such inexpressible

sufferings in obedience to God's command, and for the vindication of the honor of His authority and majesty; nor did ever any mere creature give such a testimony of love to God as that was. And yet this was the greatest expression of His love to sinful men who were enemies to God. Romans 5:10: "When we were enemies we were reconciled to God by the death of His Son." The greatness of Christ's love to such appears in nothing so much as in its being dying love. That blood of Christ which fell in great drops to the ground in His agony was shed from love to God's enemies and His own. That shame and spitting, that torment of body, and that exceeding sorrow even unto death which He endured in His soul was what He underwent from love to rebels against God, to save them from hell and purchase for them eternal glory. Never did Christ so eminently show His regard to God's honor as in offering up Himself a victim to justice. And yet in this, above all, He manifested His love to them who dishonored God so as to bring such guilt on themselves that nothing less than His blood could atone for it.

(3) Christ never so eminently appeared *for* divine justice, and yet never suffered so much *from* divine justice, as when He offered up Himself a sacrifice for our sins. In Christ's great sufferings His infinite regard to the honor of God's justice distinguishingly appeared; for it was from regard to that that He thus humbled Himself. And yet in these sufferings Christ was the mark of the vindictive expressions of that very justice of God. Avenging justice then spent all its force upon Him on account of our guilt, which made Him sweat blood and cry out upon the cross, and probably rent His vitals—broke His heart, the fountain of blood, or some other blood vessels—and by the violent fermentation turned His blood to water. For the blood and water that issued out of His side, when pierced by the spear, seems to have been ex-

travasated blood; and so there might be a kind of literal fulfillment of Psalm 22:14: "I am poured out like water, and all my bones are out of joint; my heart is like wax, it is melted in the midst of my bowels." And this was the way and means by which Christ stood up for the honor of God's justice, by thus suffering its terrible executions. For when He had undertaken for sinners, and had substituted Himself in their place, divine justice could have its due honor in no other way than by His suffering its revenges. In this the diverse excellencies that met in the person of Christ appeared: His infinite regard to God's justice, and such love to those who have exposed themselves to it as induced Him thus to yield Himself a sacrifice to it.

(4) Christ's holiness never so illustriously shone forth as it did in His last sufferings, and yet He never was to such a degree treated as guilty. Christ's holiness never had such a trial as it had then, and therefore never had so great a manifestation. When it was tried in this furnace, it came forth as gold, or as silver purified seven times. His holiness then, above all, appeared in His steadfast pursuit of the honor of God, and in His obedience to Him. For His yielding Himself unto death was transcendently the greatest act of obedience that ever was paid to God by anyone since the foundation of the world.

And yet then Christ was, in the greatest degree, treated as a wicked person would have been. He was apprehended and bound as a malefactor. His accusers represented Him as a most wicked wretch. In His sufferings before His crucifixion, He was treated as if He had been the worst and vilest of mankind; and then He was put to a kind of death that none but the worst sort of malefactors were wont to suffer, those who were most abject in their persons and guilty of the blackest crimes. And He suffered as though guilty from God Himself, by reason of our guilt imputed to Him; for He who knew no sin was made sin for us. He was made subject to wrath as if He had been sinful Himself. He was made a curse for us.

Christ never so greatly manifested His hatred of sin as against God as in His dying to take away the dishonor that sin had done to God; and yet never was He to such a degree subject to the terrible effects of God's hatred of sin and wrath against it as He was then. In this appears those diverse excellencies meeting in Christ: love to God and grace to sinners.

(5) He never was so dealt with as unworthy as in His last sufferings; and yet it is chiefly on account of them that He is accounted worthy. He was therein dealt with as if He had not been worthy to live. They cried out, "Away with Him! Away with Him! Crucify Him" (John 19:15). And they preferred Barabbas before Him. And He suffered from the Father as one whose demerits were infinite, by reason of our demerits that were laid upon Him. And yet it was especially by that act of His subjecting Himself to those sufferings that He merited, and on the account of which chiefly He was accounted worthy of, the glory of His exaltation. Philippians 2:8–9: "He humbled Himself, and became obedient unto death; wherefore God hath highly exalted Him." And we see that it is on this account chiefly that He is extolled as worthy by saints and angels in the context of our text: "Worthy," say they, "is the Lamb that was slain." This shows an admirable conjunction in Him of infinite dignity on one hand, and infinite condescension and love to the infinitely unworthy.

(6) Christ, in His last sufferings, suffered most extremely from those towards whom He was then manifesting His greatest act of love. He never suffered so much from His Father (though not from any hatred of Him, but from hatred for our sins), for He then forsook Him, or took away the comforts of His presence. And then "it pleased the Lord to bruise

Him, and put Him to grief" (Isaiah 53:10). And yet never gave He so great a manifestation of love to God as then, as has been already observed. So Christ never suffered so much from the hands of men as He did then; and yet never was He in so high an exercise of love to men. He never was so ill treated by His disciples, who were so unconcerned about His sufferings that they would not watch with Him one hour in His agony; and when He was apprehended, all forsook Him and fled except Peter, who denied Him with oaths and curses. And yet then He was suffering, shedding His blood, and pouring out His soul unto death for them. Yea, He probably was then shedding His blood for some of them who shed His blood, for whom He prayed while they were crucifying Him, and who were probably afterwards brought home to Christ by Peter's preaching (compare Luke 23:34; Acts 2:23, 36–37, 41; 3:17 and 4:4). This shows an admirable meeting of justice and grace in the redemption of Christ.

(7) It was in Christ's last sufferings, above all, that He was delivered up to the power of His enemies; and yet by these, above all, He obtained victory over His enemies. Christ never was so in His enemies' hands as in the time of His last sufferings. They sought His life before, but from time to time they were restrained, and Christ escaped out of their hands. And this reason is given for it: His time was not yet come. But now they were suffered to work their will upon Him. He was, in a great degree, delivered up to the malice and cruelty of both wicked men and devils. And therefore, when Christ's enemies came to apprehend Him, He said to them (Luke 22:53), "When I was daily with you in the temple, ye stretched forth no hand against Me; but this is your hour, and the power of darkness."

And yet it was principally by means of those sufferings that He conquered and overthrew His enemies. Christ never so effectually bruised Satan's head as when Satan bruised His heel. The weapon with which Christ warred against the devil, and obtained a most complete victory and glorious triumph over him, was the cross, the instrument and weapon with which he thought he had overthrown Christ and brought on Him shameful destruction. Colossians 2:14–15: "Blotting out the handwriting of ordinances, nailing it to His cross; and having spoiled principalities and powers, He made a show of them openly, triumphing over them in it." In His last sufferings, Christ sapped the very foundations of Satan's kingdom. He conquered His enemies in their own territories, and beat them with their own weapons, as David cut off Goliath's head with his own sword. The devil had, as it were, swallowed up Christ as the whale did Jonah; but it was deadly poison to him. He gave himself a mortal wound in his own bowels. He was soon sick of his morsel, and was forced to do by him as the whale did by Jonah. To this day he is heartsick of what he then swallowed as his prey. In those sufferings of Christ was laid the foundation of all that glorious victory He has already obtained over Satan in the overthrow of his heathenish kingdom in the Roman empire, and all the success the gospel has had since—and also of all His future and still more glorious victory that is to be obtained in the earth. Thus Samson's riddle is most eminently fulfilled in Judges 14:14: "Out of the eater came forth meat, and out of the strong came forth sweetness." And thus the true Samson does more towards the destruction of His enemies at His death than in His life. In yielding up Himself to death, He pulls down the temple of Dagon and destroys many thousands of His enemies, even while they are making themselves sport in His sufferings. And so He whose type was the ark pulls down Dagon, and breaks off his head and hands in his own temple, even while He is brought in there as Dagon's captive.

Thus Christ appeared at the same time and in the same act, as both a lion and a lamb. He appeared as a lamb in the hands of His cruel enemies, as a lamb in the paws and between the devouring jaws of a roaring lion. Yea, He was a lamb actually slain by this lion; and yet, at the same time, as the Lion of the tribe of Judah He conquers and triumphs over Satan, destroying His own devourer, as Samson did the lion that roared upon him when he rent him as he would a kid. And in nothing has Christ appeared so much as a lion, in glorious strength destroying His enemies, as when He was brought as a lamb to the slaughter. In His greatest weakness He was most strong; and when He suffered most from His enemies He brought the greatest confusion on His enemies. Thus this admirable conjunction of divers excellencies was manifest in Christ in His offering up Himself to God in His last sufferings.

4. It is still manifest in His acts, in His present state of exaltation in heaven. Indeed, in His exalted state He most eminently appears in manifestation of those excellencies, on the account of which He is compared to a lion. But still He appears as a lamb. Revelation 14:1: "And I looked, and lo, a Lion stood on Mount Zion"; as in His state of humiliation He chiefly appeared as a lamb, and yet did not appear without manifestation of His divine majesty and power as the Lion of the tribe of Judah. Though Christ is now at the right hand of God, exalted as King of heaven and Lord of the universe, yet as He still is in the human nature He still excels in humility. Though the man Christ Jesus is the highest of all creatures in heaven, yet He as much excels them all in humility as He does in glory and dignity; for none sees so much of the distance between God and Him as He does. And though He now appears in such glorious majesty and dominion in heaven, yet He appears as a lamb in His condescending, mild, and sweet treat-

ment of His saints there; for He is a Lamb still, even amidst the throne of His exaltation. And He who is the Shepherd of the whole flock is Himself a Lamb, and goes before them in heaven as such. Revelation 7:17: "For the Lamb, which is in the midst of the throne, shall feed them, and shall lead them unto living fountains of waters, and God shall wipe away all tears from their eyes." Though in heaven every knee bows to Him, and though the angels fall down before Him adoring Him, yet He treats His saints with infinite condescension, mildness, and endearment. And in His acts towards the saints on earth, He still appears as a lamb, manifesting exceeding love and tenderness in His intercession for them, as one who has had experience of affliction and temptation. He has not forgotten what these things are; nor has He forgotten how to pity those who are subject to them. And He still manifests His lamb-like excellencies in His dealings with His saints on earth in admirable forbearance, love, gentleness, and compassion. Behold Him instructing, supplying, supporting, and comforting them; often coming to them, and manifesting Himself to them by His Spirit, that He may sup with them and they with Him. Behold Him admitting them to sweet communion, enabling them with boldness and confidence to come to Him, and solacing their hearts. And in heaven Christ still appears, as it were, with the marks of His wounds upon Him; and so He appears as a Lamb as has been slain, as He was represented in the vision to St. John, in the text, when He appeared to open the book sealed with seven seals, which is part of the glory of His exaltation.

5. And last, this admirable conjunction of excellencies will be manifest in Christ's acts at the last judgment. He then, above all other times, will appear as the Lion of the tribe of Judah in infinite greatness and majesty, when He shall come in the glory of His Father with all the holy angels, and the

earth shall tremble before Him, and the hills shall melt. This is He "that shall sit on a great white throne, before whose face the earth and heaven shall flee away" (Revelation 20:11). He will then appear in the most dreadful and amazing manner to the wicked. The devils tremble at the thought of that appearance; and, when it shall be, the kings, the great men, the rich men, the chief captains, the mighty men, and every bondman and every free man shall hide themselves in the dens, and in the rocks of the mountains, and shall cry to the mountains and rocks to fall on them to hide them from the face and wrath of the Lamb. And none can declare or conceive of the amazing manifestations of wrath in which He will then appear towards these, or the trembling and astonishment, the shrieking and gnashing of teeth, with which they shall stand before His judgment seat and receive the terrible sentence of His wrath.

And yet He will at the same time appear as a Lamb to His saints. He will receive them as friends and brethren, treating them with infinite mildness and love. There shall be nothing in Him terrible to them, but towards them He will clothe Himself wholly with sweetness and endearment. The Church shall be then admitted to Him as His bride; that shall be her wedding day. The saints shall all be sweetly invited to come with Him to inherit the kingdom, and reign in it with Him to all eternity.

Application

1. From this doctrine we may learn one reason why Christ is called by such a variety of names, and held forth under such a variety of representations in Scripture. It is the better to signify and exhibit to us that variety of excellencies that meet together and are conjoined in Him. Many appellations are

mentioned together in one verse, Isaiah 9:6: "For unto us a Child is born, unto us a Son is given, and the government shall be upon His shoulder; and His name shall be called Wonderful, Counselor, the mighty God, the everlasting Father, the Prince of Peace." It shows a wonderful conjunction of excellencies that the same person should be a Son, born and given, and yet be the everlasting Father, without beginning or end; that He should be a Child, and yet be He whose name is Counselor and the mighty God. And well may His name, in whom such things are enjoined, be called "Wonderful."

By reason of the same wonderful conjunction, Christ is represented by a great variety of sensible things that are, on some account, excellent. Thus in some places He is called a Sun (Malachi 4:2), in others a Star (Numbers 24:17). And He is especially represented by the Morning-Star as being that which excels all other stars in brightness, and is the forerunner of the day (Revelation 22:16). And as, in our text, He is compared to a lion in one verse and a lamb in the next, so sometimes He is compared to a roe or a young hart, another creature most diverse from a lion. So in some places He is called a rock; in others He is compared to a pearl. In some places He is called a Man of War and the Captain of our Salvation; in other places He is represented as a bridegroom. In Song of Solomon 2:1, he is compared to a rose and lily, that are sweet and beautiful flowers; in the next verse He is compared to a tree bearing sweet fruit. In Isaiah 53:2 He is called a Root out of a dry ground; but elsewhere, instead of that, He is called the Tree of Life that grows (not in a dry or barren ground, but) "in the midst of the Paradise of God" (Revelation 2:7).

2. Let the consideration of this wonderful meeting of diverse excellencies in Christ induce you to accept Him, and

The Excellency of Christ

close with Him as your Savior. As all manner of excellencies meet in Him, so there are concurring in Him all manner of arguments and motives to move you to choose Him for your Savior, and everything that tends to encourage poor sinners to come and put their trust in Him. His fullness and all-sufficiency as a Savior gloriously appear in that variety of excellencies that has been spoken of.

Fallen man is in a state of exceedingly great misery, and is helpless in it. He is a poor, weak creature, like an infant cast out in its blood on the day that it is born. But Christ is the Lion of the tribe of Judah. He is strong, though we are weak. He has prevailed to do that for us which no other creature could do. Fallen man is a mean, despicable creature, a contemptible worm; but Christ, who has undertaken for us, is infinitely honorable and worthy. Fallen man is polluted, but Christ is infinitely holy; fallen man is hateful, but Christ is infinitely lovely; fallen man is the object of God's indignation, but Christ is infinitely dear to Him. We have dreadfully provoked God, but Christ has performed that righteousness which is infinitely precious in God's eyes.

And here is not only infinite strength and infinite worthiness, but infinite condescension, and love and mercy, as great as power and dignity. If you are a poor, distressed sinner whose heart is ready to sink for fear that God never will have mercy on you, you need not be afraid to go to Christ for fear that He is either unable or unwilling to help you. Here is a strong foundation, and an inexhaustible treasure, to answer the necessities of your poor soul; and here is infinite grace and gentleness to invite and embolden a poor, unworthy, fearful soul to come to it. If Christ accepts you, you need not fear but that you will be safe; for He is a strong Lion for your defense. And if you come, you need not fear but that you shall be accepted; for He is like a Lamb to all who come to Him, and receives them with infinite grace and tenderness.

It is true that He has awful majesty. He is the great God, and infinitely high above you. But there is this to encourage and embolden the poor sinner: that Christ is man as well as God. He is a creature as well as the Creator; and He is the most humble and lowly in heart of any creature in heaven or earth. This may well make the poor, unworthy creature bold in coming to Him. You need not hesitate one moment, but may run to Him and cast yourself upon Him. You will certainly be graciously and meekly received by Him. Though He is a lion, He will only be a lion to your enemies; but He will be a lamb to you. It could not have been conceived, had it not been so in the person of Christ, that there could have been so much in any Savior that is inviting and tends to encourage sinners to trust in Him. Whatever your circumstances are, you need not be afraid to come to such a Savior as this. Be you never so wicked a creature, here is worthiness enough; be you never so poor, mean, and ignorant a creature, there is no danger of being despised; for though He is so much greater than you, He is also immensely more humble than you. Anyone of you who is a father or mother will not despise one of your own children who comes to you in distress. Much less danger is there of Christ despising you if you, in your heart, come to Him. Here let me a little expostulate with the poor, burdened, distressed soul.

(1) What are you afraid of, that you dare not venture your soul upon Christ? Are you afraid that He cannot save you, that He is not strong enough to conquer the enemies of your soul? But how can you desire one stronger than the "mighty God," as Christ is called (Isaiah 9:6)? Is there need of greater than infinite strength? Are you afraid that He will not be willing to stoop so low as to take any gracious notice of you? But then look on Him, as He stood in the ring of

soldiers, exposing His blessed face to be buffeted and spat upon by them! Behold Him bound with His back uncovered to those who smote Him! And behold Him hanging on the cross! Do you think that He who had condescension enough to stoop to these things, and that for His crucifiers, will be unwilling to accept you if you come to Him? Or are you afraid that if He does accept you God the Father will not accept Him for you? But consider, will God reject His own Son, in whom His infinite delight is, and has been from all eternity, and who is so united to Him that if He should reject Him He would reject Himself?

(2) What is there that you can desire should be in a Savior that is not in Christ? Or wherein should you desire a Savior should be otherwise than Christ is? What excellency is there wanting? What is there that is great or good? What is there that is venerable or winning? What is there that is adorable or endearing; or, what can you think of that would be encouraging which is not to be found in the person of Christ? Would you have your Savior to be great and honorable because you are not willing to be beholden to a mean person? And is not Christ a person honorable enough to be worthy that you should be dependent on Him? Is He not a person high enough to be appointed to so honorable a work as your salvation? Would you not only have a Savior of high degree, but would you have Him, notwithstanding His exaltation and dignity, to be made also of low degree that He might have experience of afflictions and trials, that He might learn by the things that He has suffered, to pity those who suffer and are tempted? And has not Christ been made low enough for you? And has He not suffered enough? Would you not only have Him possess experience of the afflictions you now suffer, but also of that amazing wrath that you fear hereafter, that He may know how to pity those who are in

danger and are afraid of it? This Christ has had experience of, which experience gave Him a thousand times greater sense of it than you have, or any man living has.

Would you have your Savior to be one who is near to God, that His mediation might be prevalent with Him? And can you desire Him to be nearer to God than Christ is, who is His only-begotten Son, of the same essence with the Father? And would you not only have Him near to God, but also near to you, that you may have free access to Him? And would you have Him nearer to you than to be in the same nature, united to you by a spiritual union, so close as to be fitly represented by the union of the wife to the husband, of the branch to the vine, of the member to the head; yea, so as to be one spirit? For so He will be united to you if you accept Him. Would you have a Savior who has given some great and extraordinary testimony of mercy and love to sinners by something that He has done as well as by what He says? And can you think or conceive of greater things than Christ has done? Was it not a great thing for Him who was God to take upon Himself human nature, to be not only God, but man thenceforward to all eternity? But would you look upon suffering for sinners to be a yet greater testimony of love to sinners than merely doing, though it be ever so extraordinary a thing that He has done? And would you desire that a Savior should suffer more than Christ has suffered for sinners? What is there wanting, or what would you add if you could, to make Him more fit to be your Savior? But further, to induce you to accept Christ as your Savior, consider two things particularly:

[1] How much Christ appears as the Lamb of God in His invitations to you to come to Him and trust in Him. With what sweet grace and kindness does He, from time to time, call and invite you! Proverbs 8:4: "Unto you, O men, I call, and My voice is to the sons of men." And Isaiah 55:1: "Ho,

The Excellency of Christ

every one that thirsteth, come ye to the waters, and he that hath no money, come ye, buy and eat; yea, come, buy wine and milk without money, and without price." How gracious is He here in inviting everyone who thirsts, and in so repeating His invitation over and over: "Come ye to the waters; come, buy and eat; yea, come!" Mark the excellency of that entertainment which He invites you to accept: "Come, buy wine and milk!" Your poverty, having nothing to pay for it, shall be no objection. "Come, he that hath no money, come without money, and without price!" What gracious arguments and expostulations He uses with you! "Wherefore do ye spend money for that which is not bread? and your labor for that which satisfieth not? Hearken diligently unto Me, and eat ye that which is good, and let your soul delight itself in fatness" (verse 2). It is as much as if to say, "It is altogether needless for you to continue laboring and toiling for that which can never serve your turn, seeking rest in the world and in your own righteousness. I have made abundant provision for you of that which is really good, and will fully satisfy your desires, answer your end, and stand ready to accept you. You need not be afraid. If you will come to Me, I will engage to see all your wants supplied, and you made a happy creature."

He promises in the third verse, "Incline your ear, and come unto Me; hear, and your soul shall live, and I will make an everlasting covenant with you, even the sure mercies of David." And in Proverbs 9:4, how gracious and sweet is the invitation there! "Whoso is simple, let him turn in hither." Let you be never so poor, ignorant, and blind a creature, you shall be welcome. And in the following verse, Christ sets forth the provision that He has made for you: "Come, eat of My bread, and drink of the wine which I have mingled." You are in a poor, famished state, and have nothing wherewith to feed your perishing soul; you have been seeking something, but yet remain destitute. Hearken how Christ calls you to eat of His bread, and to drink of the wine that He has mingled! And how much like a lamb does Christ appear in Matthew 11:28–30: "Come unto Me, all ye that labor and are heavy laden, and I will give you rest. Take My yoke upon you, and learn of Me, for I am meek and lowly in heart; and ye shall find rest to your souls. For My yoke is easy, and My burden is light."

O you poor, distressed soul! Whoever you are, consider that Christ mentions your very case when He calls to those who labor and are heavy laden! How He repeatedly promises you rest if you come to Him! In the 28th verse He says, "I will give you rest." And in the 29th verse, "Ye shall find rest to your souls." This is what you want. This is the thing you have been so long in vain seeking after. Oh, how sweet would rest be to you if you could but obtain it! Come to Christ, and you *shall* obtain it! And hear how Christ, to encourage you, represents Himself as a lamb! He tells you that He is meek and lowly in heart; and are you afraid to come to such a one? And again in Revelation 3:20: "Behold, I stand at the door and knock; if any man hear My voice, and open the door, I will come in to him, and I will sup with him, and he with Me." Christ condescends not only to call you to Himself, but He comes to you. He comes to your door and there knocks. He might send an officer and seize you as a rebel and a vile malefactor; but instead of that He comes and knocks at your door, and seeks that you would receive Him into your house as your Friend and Savior. And He not only knocks at your door, but He stands there waiting while you are backward and unwilling. And not only so, but He makes promises as to what He will do for you if you will admit Him, and what privileges He will admit you to: He will sup with you, and you with Him. And again in Revelation 22:16–17: "I am the root and the offspring of David, and the bright and morning star. And the

The Excellency of Christ

Spirit and the bride say, 'Come.' And let him that heareth say, 'Come.' And let him that is athirst come. And whosoever will, let him take of the water of life freely." How does Christ here graciously set before you His own winning, attractive excellency! And how does He condescend to declare to you not only His own invitation, but the invitation of the Spirit and the bride, if by any means He might encourage you to come! And how does He invite everyone who will that they may "take of the water of life freely," that they may take it as a free gift, however precious it is, and though it is the water of life!

[2] If you do come to Christ, He will appear as a Lion, in His glorious power and dominion, to defend you. All those excellencies of His in which He appears as a lion shall be yours, and shall be employed for you in your defense, for your safety, and to promote your glory. He will be as a lion to fight against your enemies. He who touches you or offends you will provoke His wrath, as he who stirs up a lion. Unless your enemies can conquer this Lion, they shall not be able to destroy or hurt you; unless they are stronger than He, they shall not be able to hinder your happiness. Isaiah 31:4: "For thus hath the Lord spoken unto me, 'Like as the lion and the young lion roaring on his prey, when a multitude of shepherds is called forth against him, he will not be afraid of their voice, nor abase himself for the noise of them; so shall the Lord of hosts come down to fight for Mount Zion, and for the hill thereof.'"

3. Let what has been said be improved to induce you to love the Lord Jesus Christ, and choose Him for your friend and portion. As there is such an admirable meeting of diverse excellencies in Christ, so there is everything in Him to render Him worthy of your love and choice, and to win and engage it. Whatsoever there is or can be desirable in a friend is in Christ, and that to the highest degree that can be desired.

Would you choose for a friend a person of great dignity? It is an attractive thing with men to have those for their friends who are much above them, because they look upon themselves honored by the friendship of such. Thus, how attractive would it be to an inferior maid to be the object of the dear love of some great and excellent prince. But Christ is infinitely above you, and above all the princes of the earth, for He is the King of kings. So honorable a person as this offers Himself to you in the nearest and dearest friendship.

And would you choose to have a friend not only great but good? In Christ infinite greatness and infinite goodness meet together, and receive luster and glory one from another. His greatness is rendered lovely by His goodness. The greater anyone is without goodness, so much the greater evil; but when infinite goodness is joined with greatness, it renders it a glorious and adorable greatness. So, on the other hand, His infinite goodness receives luster from His greatness. He who is of great understanding and ability, and is withal of a good and excellent disposition, is deservedly more esteemed than a lower and lesser being with the same kind of inclination and good will. Indeed, goodness is excellent in whatever subject it is found; it is beauty and excellency itself and renders all excellent that are possessed of it, and yet most excellent when joined with greatness. The very same excellent qualities of gold render the body in which they are inherent more precious and of greater value when joined with greater than when with lesser dimensions. And how glorious is the sight to see Him who is the great Creator and supreme Lord of heaven and earth, full of condescension, tender pity, and mercy, towards the mean and unworthy! His almighty power and infinite majesty and self-sufficiency render His exceeding love and grace the more surprising. And how do His condescension and compassion endear His majesty, power, and

The Excellency of Christ

dominion, and render those attributes pleasant that would otherwise be only terrible! Would you not desire that your friend, though great and honorable, should be of such condescension and grace, and so to have the way opened to free access to him, that his exaltation above you might not hinder your free enjoyment of his friendship? And would you choose not only that the infinite greatness and majesty of your friend should be, as it were, mollified and sweetened with condescension and grace; but would you also desire to have your friend brought nearer to you? Would you choose a friend far above you, and yet, as it were, upon a level with you too? Though it is attractive to men to have a near and dear friend of superior dignity, yet there is also an inclination in them to have their friend be a sharer with them in circumstances. Thus is Christ. Though He is the great God, yet He has, as it were, brought Himself down to be upon a level with you so as to become man as you are, that He might not only be your Lord, but your brother, and that He might be the more fit to be a companion for such a worm of the dust. This is one end of Christ's taking upon Himself man's nature: that His people might gain the advantage of a more familiar conversation with Him than the infinite distance of the divine nature would allow of. And upon this account the Church longed for Christ's incarnation in Song of Solomon 8:1: "Oh, that thou wert as my brother, that sucked the breasts of my mother! when I should find thee without, I would kiss thee, yea, I should not be despised."

One design of God in the gospel is to bring us to make God the object of our undivided respect, that He may engross our regard in every way, that whatever natural inclination there is in our souls He may be the center of it; that God may be all in all. But there is an inclination in the creature not only to the adoration of a Lord and Sovereign, but to complacency in some one as a friend, to love and delight in someone who may be conversed with as a companion. And virtue and holiness do not destroy or weaken this inclination of our nature. But so has God contrived in the affair of our redemption that a divine person may be the object even of this inclination of our nature. And in order hereto, such a one has come down to us, and has taken our nature, and has become one of us, and calls Himself our friend, brother, and companion. Psalm 122:8: "For my brethren and companions' sake, I will now say, 'Peace be within thee.' "

But is it not enough in order to invite and encourage you to free access to a friend so great and high, that He is one of infinite condescending grace, and also has taken your own nature, and is become man? But would you further, to embolden and win you, have him a man of wonderful meekness and humility? Why, such a one is Christ! He has not only become man for you, but by far the meekest and most humble of all men, the greatest instance of these sweet virtues that ever was or will be. And beside these, He has all other human excellencies in the highest perfection. These, indeed, are no proper addition to His divine excellencies. Christ has no more excellency in His person since His incarnation than He had before; for divine excellency is infinite and cannot be added to. Yet His human excellencies are additional manifestations of His glory and excellency to us, and are additional recommendations of Him to our esteem and love, who are of finite comprehension. Though His human excellencies are but communications and reflections of His divine, and though this light, as reflected, falls infinitely short of the divine fountain of light in its immediate glory, yet the reflection shines not without its proper advantages as presented to our view and affection. The glory of Christ, as it appears in His divinity, though far brighter, more dazzles our eyes, and exceeds the strength of our sight or our comprehension; but, as it shines in the human excellencies of Christ, it is brought more to a level with our conceptions, and suitableness to our nature and manner, yet retaining a semblance of the same divine beauty and a savor of the same divine sweetness. But as both divine and human excellencies meet together in Christ, they set off and recommend each other to us. It tends to endear the divine majesty and holiness of Christ to us that these are attributes of one in our nature, one of us who has become our brother, and is the meekest and humblest of men. It encourages us to look upon these divine perfections, however high and great, since we have some near concern in, and liberty freely to enjoy them. And, on the other hand, how much more glorious and surprising do the meekness, humility, obedience, resignation, and other human excellencies of Christ appear when we consider that they are in so great a person as the eternal Son of God, the Lord of heaven and earth!

By choosing Christ for your friend and portion, you will obtain these two infinite benefits:

1. Christ will give Himself to you, with all those various excellencies that meet in Him, to your full and everlasting enjoyment. He will ever after treat you as His dear friend; and you shall ere long be where He is, and shall behold His glory, and dwell with Him in most free and intimate communion and enjoyment.

When the saints get to heaven, they shall not merely see Christ, and have to do with Him as subjects and servants with a glorious and gracious Lord and Sovereign, but Christ will entertain them as friends and brethren. This we may learn from the manner of Christ's conversing with His disciples here on earth: though He was their sovereign Lord, and did not refuse, but required, their supreme respect and adoration, yet He did not treat them as earthly sovereigns are wont to do their subjects. He did not keep them at an awful distance, but all along conversed with them with the most friendly familiarity, as a father among a company of children, yea, as with brethren. So He did with the twelve, and so He did with Mary, Martha, and Lazarus. He told His disciples that He did not call them servants, but friends; and we read of one of them who leaned on His bosom. Doubtless He will not treat His disciples with less freedom and endearment in heaven. He will not keep them at a greater distance for His being in a state of exaltation, but He will rather take them into a state of exaltation with Him. This will be the improvement Christ will make of His own glory, to make His beloved friends partakers with Him, to glorify them in His glory, as He says to His Father in John 17:22–23: "And the glory which Thou hast given Me, have I given them, that they may be one, even as we are one; I in them . . . ." We are to consider that, though Christ is greatly exalted, He is exalted not as a private person for Himself only, but as His people's head. He is exalted in their name and upon their account as the first fruits, and as representing the whole harvest. He is not exalted that He may be at a greater distance from them, but that they may be exalted with Him. The exaltation and honor of the head is not to make a greater distance between the head and the members, but the members have the same relation and union with the head they had before, and are honored with the head. And instead of the distance being greater, the union shall be nearer and more perfect. When believers get to heaven, Christ will conform them to Himself. As He is set down in His Father's throne, so they shall sit down with Him on His throne, and shall in their measure be made like Him.

When Christ was going to heaven, He comforted His disciples with the thought that, after awhile, He would come again and take them to Himself, that they might be with Him. And we are not to suppose that when the disciples got to heaven, they found Him keeping a greater distance than He used to do. No, doubtless, He embraced them as friends, and welcomed them to His and their Father's house, and to His and their glory. They who had been His friends in this world, who had been together with Him here, and had together partaken of sorrows and troubles, are now welcomed by Him to rest, and to partake of glory with Him. He took them and led them into His chambers, and showed them all His glory; as He prayed in John 17:24: "Father, I will that they also, whom Thou hast given Me, be with Me, that they may behold the glory which Thou hast given Me." He led them to His living fountains of waters, and made them partake of His delights; as He prays in John 17:13: "That My joy may be fulfilled in themselves." He sat them down with Him at His table in His kingdom, and made them partake with Him of His dainties, according to His promise (Luke 22:30). He led them into His banqueting house, and enabled them to drink new wine with Him in the kingdom of His heavenly Father, as He foretold them when He instituted the Lord's Supper (Matthew 26:29).

Yea, the saints' conversation with Christ in heaven shall not only be as intimate, and their access to Him as free, as of the disciples on earth, but in many respects much more so. For in heaven that vital union shall be perfect which is exceedingly imperfect here. While the saints are in this world, there are great remains of sin and darkness to separate or disunite them from Christ, which shall then all be removed. This is not a time for that full acquaintance and those glorious manifestations of love which Christ designs for His people hereafter. This seems to be signified by His speech to Mary Magdalene, when ready to embrace Him, when she met Him after His resurrection. John 20:17: "Jesus saith unto her,

'Touch Me not, for I am not yet ascended to My Father.' "

When the saints shall see Christ's glory and exaltation in heaven, it will indeed possess their hearts with the greater admiration and adoring respect; it will not awe them into any separation, but will serve only to heighten their surprise and joy when they find Christ condescending to admit them to such intimate access, and so freely and fully communicating Himself to them. So that if we choose Christ for our friend and portion, we shall hereafter be so received to Him that there shall be nothing to hinder the fullest enjoyment of Him to satisfy the utmost cravings of our souls. We may take our full swing at gratifying our spiritual appetite after these holy pleasures. Christ will then say, as in Song of Solomon 5:1, "Eat, O friends, drink, yea, drink abundantly, O beloved." And this shall be our entertainment to all eternity! There shall never be any end of this happiness, or anything to interrupt our enjoyment of it, or in the least to molest us in it!

2. By our being united to Christ, we have a more glorious union with, and enjoyment of, God the Father than otherwise could be. For hereby the saints' relation to God becomes much nearer; they are the children of God in a higher manner than otherwise could be. For, being members of God's own Son, they are in a sort partakers of His relation to the Father. They are not only sons of God by regeneration, but by a kind of communion in the sonship of the eternal Son. This seems to be intended in Galatians 4:4–6: "God sent forth His Son, made of a woman, made under the law, to redeem them that are under the law, that we might receive the adoption of sons. And because ye are sons, God hath sent forth the Spirit of His Son into your hearts, crying, 'Abba, Father.' " The Church is the daughter of God, not only as He has begotten her by His Word and Spirit, but as she is the spouse of His eternal Son.

The Excellency of Christ

So we, being members of the Son, are partakers in our measure of the Father's love to the Son and complacence in Him. John 17:23: "I in them, and Thou in Me . . . Thou hast loved them as Thou hast loved Me." And verse 26: "That the love wherewith Thou hast loved Me may be in them." And John 16:27: "The Father Himself loveth you, because ye have loved Me, and have believed that I came out from God." So we shall, according to our capacities, be partakers of the Son's enjoyment of God, and have His joy fulfilled in ourselves (John 17:13). And by this means we shall come to an immensely higher, more intimate and full enjoyment of God than otherwise could have been. For there is, doubtless, an infinite intimacy between the Father and the Son which is expressed by His being in the bosom of the Father. And the saints being in Him shall, in their measure and manner, partake with Him in it, and of the blessedness of it.

And thus is the affair of our redemption ordered, that thereby we are brought to an immensely more exalted kind of union with God and enjoyment of Him, both the Father and the Son, than otherwise could have been. Since Christ is united to the human nature, we have advantage for a more free and full enjoyment of Him than we could have had if He had remained only in the divine nature. So again, we being united to a divine person as His members can have a more intimate union and intercourse with God the Father, who is only in the divine nature, than otherwise could be. Christ, who is a divine person, by taking on Himself our nature, descends from the infinite distance and height above us, and is brought nigh to us, whereby we have advantage for the full enjoyment of Him. And, on the other hand, we, by being in Christ, a divine person, do, as it were, ascend up to God through the infinite distance, and have hereby advantage for the full enjoyment of Him also.

This was the design of Christ, that He, His Father, and His people might all be united in one. John 17:21–23: "That they all may be one, as Thou, Father, art in Me, and I in Thee; that they also may be one in us, that the world may believe that Thou hast sent Me. And the glory which Thou hast given Me, I have given them, that they may be one, even as we are one; I in them and Thou in Me, that they may be made perfect in one." Christ has brought it to pass that those whom the Father has given Him should be brought into the household of God; that He, His Father, and His people should be as one society, one family, so that the Church should be, as it were, admitted into the society of the blessed Trinity.

Christ Exalted

*Jesus Christ Gloriously Exalted Above All
Evil in the Work of Redemption*

"For He must reign, till He hath put all enemies under His feet. The last enemy that shall be destroyed is death."

1 Corinthians 15:25–26

The Apostle in this chapter particularly opposes some among the Corinthian Christian who denied the resurrection of the dead, and infested the church with their doctrine. There were two sorts of persons in that age who were especially great opposers of the doctrine of the resurrection: one among the Jews and the other among the heathen. Among the Jews were the Sadducees, of whom we read in Acts 23:8, "For the Sadducees say that there is no resurrection, either angel or spirit," and we have the same account in other places. Among the heathen, the chief opposers of this doctrine were their philosophers. The doctrine of the resurrection of the dead was not consistent with their philosophy, by the principles of which it was impossible that one who was deprived of the habit of life should ever receive it again. And therefore they ridiculed the doctrine when the Apostle preached it among them at Athens (Acts 17). Probably the church at Corinth received this corruption from the philosophers, and not the Sadducees. For Corinth was near to Athens, the place of the chief resort of the philosophers of Greece.

The Apostle, in opposing this error, first insists on Christ's resurrection from the dead, and next on the resurrection of all the saints at the end of the world. And in the verses just before the text, he shows how both are connected, or that one arises or follows from the other. And then he adds, "then cometh the end, when He shall have delivered up the kingdom to God, even the Father; when He shall have put down all rule and all authority and power. For He must reign till He hath put all enemies under His feet. The last enemy that shall be destroyed is death." Observe:

1. Here is one thing wherein appears the glory of that exaltation and dominion that Christ has as our Redeemer: that it issues in the subjection of all enemies under His feet. It is not said all *His* enemies, possibly because those who shall be put under His feet are not only His enemies, but also the enemies of His Father and His people. Their being under His feet denotes their being perfectly subdued, and His being gloriously exalted over them. It shall be thus with respect to God's, His, and His people's enemies universally, not one excepted. This universality is signified here in two ways: all enemies, and the very last enemy. When there shall be but one enemy left, that shall also be put under His feet.

2. We may learn what is here meant by "enemies" by the particular instance here given as the last that shall be destroyed, death. This shows that by "enemies" is not meant persons only who set themselves in opposition to God and His people, but evils; whatever is against God and His people, and opposes Christ or His saints, whether they are persons or things.

SECTION 1: How evil of all kinds has prevailed and highly exalted itself in the world.

Evil of all kinds has risen to an exceeding height in the world, and highly exalted itself against God, Christ, and the Church. This will appear by the following particulars:

Christ Exalted

1. Satan has highly exalted himself and greatly prevailed. He is vastly superior, in his natural capacity and abilities, to mankind. He was originally one of the highest rank of creatures, but proudly exalted himself, in rebellion, against God in heaven. We are told that pride was the condemnation of the devil (1 Timothy 3:6). He became proud of his own superior dignity and mighty abilities, and the glory which his Creator had put upon him, and probably thought it too much to submit to the Son of God, and attempted to exalt his throne above Him. And he prevailed to draw vast multitudes of the heavenly hosts into an open rebellion against God.

And after he was cast down from heaven, he proudly exalted himself in this world, and prevailed to do great things. By his subtle temptations he procured the fall of our first parents, and so brought about the ruin of their whole race. He procured their ruin in body and soul, and the death of both, and that they should be exposed to all manner of calamity in this world, and to eternal ruin hereafter. He so far prevailed that he drew men off from the service of their Maker and set up himself to be the god of this world; and in a little time he drew the world into that almost universal corruption which brought on the flood of waters by which it was destroyed. After that, he drew off all nations except the posterity of Jacob from the worship of the true God, darkened all the world with heathenism, and held them under this darkness for a great many ages. He himself being worshipped as god almost all over the world, the nations of the earth offered sacrifices to him and multitudes offered up their children. And during that time he often so far prevailed against the people of God that he had almost swallowed them up. The Church was often brought to the very brink of ruin.

And when Christ Himself appeared in the world, how did Satan exalt himself against Him! And he prevailed so far as to influence men to hate and despise Him all the days of His life. At last he persuaded one of His own disciples to betray Him. Accordingly, He was delivered into the hands of men to be mocked, buffeted, spat upon, and treated with the greatest ignominy that unrestrained malice could devise. At last he procured that He should be put to the most cruel and ignominious kind of death. And since then, he has greatly exalted himself against the gospel and kingdom of Christ. He has procured that the Church, for the most part, has been the subject of great persecution; has often brought it to the brink of utter destruction; has accomplished great works in setting up those great kingdoms of antichrist and Mohammed, and darkened a great part of the world that was once enlightened with the gospel of Christ with worse than heathen darkness. And he has infected the Christian world with multitudes of heresies and false ways of worship, and greatly promoted atheism and infidelity. Thus highly has the devil exalted himself against God, Christ, and the elect; and so far he has prevailed.

2. Guilt is another evil which has come to a great height in the world. All guilt is an evil of a dreadful nature. The least degree of it is enough to utterly undo any creature. It is a thing that reaches unto heaven, cries to God, and brings down His wrath. The guilt of any one sin is so terrible an evil that it prevails to bind over the guilty person to suffer everlasting burnings, and so is in some respect infinite in that it obliges to that punishment which has no end—and so is infinitely terrible. But this kind of evil has risen to a most amazing height in this world where not only *some* persons are guilty, but all in all nations and ages are naturally guilty wretches. And they who live to act any time in the world are not only guilty of one sin, but of thousands and thousands of thousands. What multiplied and what aggravated sins are some men guilty of! What guilt lies on some particular per-

sons! How much more on some particular populous cities! How much more still on this wicked world! How much does the guilt of the world transcend all account, all expression, all powers of numbers or measures! And above all, how vast is the guilt of the world in all ages, from the beginning to the end of it! To what a pitch has guilt risen! The world is, as it were, on every side loaded with it as with mountains heaped on mountains above the clouds and stars of heaven.

And guilt, when it was imputed to Christ, greatly prevailed against Him—though He was in Himself innocent, and the eternal Son of God—even so as to hold Him prisoner of justice for awhile, and to open the floodgates of God's wrath upon Him, and bring His waves and billows over Him.

3. Corruption and wickedness of heart is another thing that has risen to an exceeding height in the world. Sin has so far prevailed that it has become universal: all mere men have become sinful and corrupt creatures. Let us attend to St. Paul's description of the world in Romans 3:9–18: "Jews and Gentiles are all under sin. As it is written, 'There is none righteous, no, not one; there is none that understandeth, there is none that seeketh after God. They are all gone out of the way, they are together become unprofitable, there is none that doeth good, no not one.'" And not only is everyone corrupt, but they are all over corrupt—in every power, faculty, and principle; every part is depraved. This is here represented by the several parts of the body being corrupt, such as the throat, the tongue, the lips, the mouth, and the feet. "Their throat is an open sepulcher; with their tongues they have used deceit, the poison of asps is under their lips; whose mouth is full of cursing and bitterness; their feet are swift to shed blood." And not only is every part corrupt, but exceedingly corrupt—being possessed with dreadful principles of corruption, horribly evil dispositions and principles of sin that may be represented by

the poison of asps, which makes men like vipers and devils: principles of all uncleanness, pride, deceit, injustice, enmity, malice, blasphemy, murder. Here their throats are compared to an open sepulcher, and their mouth is said to be full of cursing and bitterness; destruction and misery are said to be in their ways.

And there are those principles of sin that are not only very bad, but every kind; there is no sort of wickedness but there is a seed of it in men. And these seeds and principles have not only a place in men's hearts, but are there in great strength. They have the absolute possession and dominion over men, so that they are sold under sin. Yea, wicked principles, and those only, are in the heart. The imagination of the thoughts of their heart is evil only. There are bad principles only, and no good ones. "There is no fear of God before their eyes." Thus the hearts of all men are "deceitful and desperately wicked" (Jeremiah 17:9).

And if we look not only at the natural corruption of the heart, but at the contracted habits of sin by wicked education and customs, how full shall we find the world of wickedness in this respect! How have men, by bad customs in sinning, broken down all restraints upon natural corruption and, as it were, abandoned themselves to wickedness! So far has corruption and wickedness prevailed in the world, and so high has it risen, that it is become a great and universal deluge that overtakes all things, and prevails with that strength so that it is like the raging waves of the tempestuous ocean which are ready to bear down all before them.

4. Many of the devil's instruments have greatly prevailed, and have been exalted to an exceeding height in the world. It has been so in almost all ages of the world. Many of the devil's instruments have prospered and prevailed till they have gotten to the head of great kingdoms and empires, with vast

riches and mighty power.

Those four great heathen monarchies that rose in the world before Christ (Babylonian, Persian, Grecian, and Roman monarchies) are spoken of in Scripture as kingdoms set up in opposition to the kingdom of Christ. So they are represented in the interpretation of Nebuchadnezzar's dream (Daniel 2:36–45). These monarchies were exceedingly powerful. The last two ruled over the greater part of the then-known world. And the last especially, the Roman empire, was exceedingly mighty, so that it is said to be different from all kingdoms, and that it should devour the whole earth, tread it down, and break it in pieces (Daniel 7:23). It is represented by the fourth beast, which was dreadful and terrible, exceedingly strong, and had great iron teeth that devoured and broke in pieces, and stamped the residue with his feet (Daniel 7:7). These four kingdoms all persecuted the Church of God in their turns, especially the last. One of the governors of this monarchy put Christ to death. And afterwards, one emperor after another made dreadful havoc of the Church, making a business of it with the force of all the empire to torment and destroy the Christians, endeavoring, if possible, to root out the Christian name from under heaven.

And in these latter ages, how have those two great instruments of the devil (antichrist and Mohammed) prevailed, and to what a pitch of advancement have they arrived, ruling over vast empires and mighty wealth, pride and power. The earth has been, as it were, subdued by them. Antichrist has set up himself as the vicar of Christ, and has for many ages usurped the power of God, "sitting in the temple of God, and showing himself that he is God; and exalting himself above all that is called God, or that is worshipped." And how dreadfully has he ravaged the Church of God, being drunk with the blood of the saints and the martyrs of Jesus. He has often, as it were, deluged the world in Christian blood, shed with the utmost cruelty that human wit and malice could invent. And, at this day, many other instruments of the devil, many heretics, atheists, and other infidels, are exerting themselves against Christ and His Church with great pride and contempt.

5. Affliction and misery have also prevailed and risen to an unspeakable height in the world. The spiritual misery which the elect are naturally in is great. They are miserable captives of sin and Satan, and under obligations to suffer eternal burnings. This misery all mankind is naturally in. And spiritual troubles and sorrows have often risen to a great height in the elect. The troubles of a wounded spirit and guilty conscience have been felt with intolerable and insupportable weight. "A wounded spirit who can bear?" (Proverbs 18:14). And the darkness that has risen to God's people after conversion, through the temptations and buffetings of the devil, and the hidings of God's face and manifestations of His anger, has been very terrible. And temporal afflictions have often risen exceedingly high. The Church of God has, for the most part, all along been a seat of great affliction and tribulation.

But as for the height to which the evil of affliction has risen, nowhere does it appear so much as in the afflictions that Christ suffered. The evil of affliction and sorrow exalted itself so high as to seize the Son of God Himself, cause Him to be all in a bloody sweat, and make His soul exceedingly sorrowful, even unto death. It caused Him to cry out, "My God, My God, why hast Thou forsaken Me?" Affliction never prevailed to such a degree in this world as in Christ, whose soul was, as it were, overwhelmed in an ocean of it.

6. Death is an evil which has greatly prevailed and made dreadful havoc in this world. How does it waste and devour mankind, one age after another, sparing none, high or low, rich or poor, good or bad! Wild beasts have destroyed many;

many cruel princes have taken away the lives of thousands, and laid waste whole countries. But death devours all; none are suffered to escape. And the bodies of the saints as well as others fall prey to this great devourer. Yea, so high did this enemy rise, that he took hold on Christ Himself, and swallowed Him among the rest. He became the prey of this great, insatiable monster. By this means was His bodily frame destroyed and laid dead in the dark and silent grave. And death still goes on destroying thousands every day. And therefore the grave is one of those things which Agur says never has enough (Proverbs 30:16). So have evils of every kind prevailed, and to such a degree have they exalted themselves in the world.

SECTION 2: How Jesus Christ, in the work of redemption, appears gloriously above all these evils.

It was not the will of the infinitely wise and holy Governor of the world that things should remain in this confusion, this reign of evil which had prevailed and exalted itself to such a height. But He had a design of subduing it, delivering an elect part of the world from it, exalting them to the possession of the greatest good, and to reign in the highest glory, out of a state of subjection to all these evils. He chose His Son as the person most fit for an undertaking that was infinitely too great for any mere creature; and He has undertaken the work of our redemption. And though these evils are so many and so great, have prevailed to such a degree, have risen to such a height, and have been, as it were, all combined together, yet wherein they have exalted themselves, Christ, in the work of redemption, appears above them. He has gloriously prevailed against them all, brings them under His feet, and rides forth in the chariots of salvation over their heads, or leading them in triumph at His chariot wheels. He appears in this work infinitely higher and mightier than they, sufficient to carry His people above them, and utterly to destroy them all.

1. Christ appears gloriously above all evil in what He did to procure redemption for us in His state of humiliation, by the righteousness He wrought out and the atonement He made for sin. The evils mentioned never seemed so much to prevail against Him as in His sufferings, but in them the foundation was laid for their overthrow. In them He appeared above Satan. Though Satan never exalted himself so high as he did in procuring these sufferings of Christ, yet then Christ laid the foundation for the utter overthrow of his kingdom. He slew Satan, as it were, with his own weapon. The spiritual David cut off this Goliath's head with his own sword, and He triumphed over him in His cross. "Having spoiled principalities and powers, He made a show of them openly, triumphing over them in it" (Colossians 2:15), in His cross, mentioned in the preceding words. Then the wisdom of Christ appeared gloriously above the subtlety of Satan. Satan, that old serpent, used a great deal of subtlety to procure Christ's death; and doubtless, when he had accomplished it, he thought he had obtained a complete victory, being then ignorant of the contrivance of our redemption. But the wisdom of Christ so ordered things that Satan's subtlety and malice should be made the very means of undermining the foundations of his kingdom; and so He wisely led him into the pit that he had dug.

In this also Christ appeared gloriously above the guilt of men. For He offered a sacrifice that was sufficient to do away with all the guilt of the whole world. Though the guilt of man was like the great mountains whose heads are lifted up to the heavens, yet His dying love and His merits appeared as a mighty deluge that overflowed the highest mountains; or like a boundless ocean that swallows them up; or like an immense

Christ Exalted

fountain of light that, with the fullness and abundance of its brightness, swallows up men's greatest sins as little motes are swallowed up and hidden in the disk of the sun.

In this Christ appeared above all the corruption of man, in that hereby He purchased holiness for the chief of sinners. And Christ, in undergoing such extreme affliction, got the victory over all misery, and laid a foundation for its being utterly abolished with respect to His elect. In dying He became the plague and destruction of death. When death slew Him, it slew itself; for Christ, through death, destroyed him who had the power of death, even the devil (Hebrews 2:14). By this He laid the foundation of the glorious resurrection of all His people to an immortal life.

2. Christ appears gloriously exalted above all evil in His resurrection and ascension into heaven. When Christ rose from the dead, then it appeared that He was above death, which, though it had taken Him captive, could not hold Him.

Then He appeared above the devil. Then this leviathan that had swallowed Him was forced to vomit Him up again; as the Philistines who had taken captive the ark were forced to return it—Dagon being fallen before it, with his head and hands broken off, and only the stumps left. Then He appeared above our guilt; for He was justified in His resurrection (Romans 4:25). In His resurrection He appeared above all affliction. For though He had been subject to much affliction, and overwhelmed in it, He then emerged out of it as having gotten the victory, never to conflict with any more sorrow.

When He ascended up into heaven, He rose far above the reach of the devil and all his instruments, who had before had Him in their hands. And now has He sat down at the right hand of God, being made Head over all things to the Church, in order to secure a complete and perfect victory over sin,

Satan, death, and all His enemies. It was then said to Him, "Sit Thou at my right hand, until I make Thine enemies Thy footstool" (Psalm 110:1). He entered into a state of glory wherein He is exalted far above all these evils, as the forerunner of His people, and to make intercession for them till they also are brought to be with Him, in like manner exalted above all evil.

3. Christ appears gloriously above all evil in His work in the hearts of the elect, in their conversion and sanctification. This is what the application of redemption, so far as it is applied in this world, consists in, which is done by the Holy Ghost as the Spirit of Christ. In this work of Christ in the hearts of His elect, He appears gloriously above Satan. For the strong man armed is overcome, and all his armor wherein he trusted is taken from him, and his spoil divided. In this work, the lamb is, by the spiritual David, taken out of the mouth of the lion and bear; the poor captive is delivered from his mighty and cruel enemies.

In this Christ appears gloriously above the corruption and wickedness of the heart; above its natural darkness in dispelling it and letting in light, and above its enmity and opposition, by prevailing over it, drawing it powerfully and irresistibly to Himself, and turning a heart of stone into a heart of flesh. He is above the obstinacy and perverseness of the will by making them willing in the day of His power. In this He appears above all their lusts. For all sin is mortified in this work, and the soul is delivered from the power and dominion of it. In this work the grace of Christ gloriously triumphs over men's guilt. He comes over the mountains of their sins and visits them with His salvation.

And God is wont often in this work, either in the beginning or progress of it, to give His people those spiritual comforts in which He gloriously appears to be above all affliction and sorrow. He often gives them to triumph over the devil and his powerful and cruel instruments. Many saints, by the influences of Christ's Spirit on their hearts, have rejoiced and triumphed when suffering the greatest torments and cruelties of their persecutors. And in this work Christ sometimes gloriously appears above death, in carrying His people far above the fears of it, and making them say, "O death, where is thy sting? O grave, where is thy victory?"

4. Christ gloriously appears above all these afore-mentioned evils in His glorifying the souls of departed saints in heaven. In this He gives a glorious victory over death. Death by it is turned from an enemy into a servant; and their death, by the glorious change that passes in the state of their souls, becomes a resurrection, rather than a death. Now Christ exalts the soul to a state of glory, wherein it is perfectly delivered from Satan and all his temptations, and all his instruments; from all remains of sin and corruption, and from all affliction. "They shall hunger no more, neither thirst any more, neither shall the sun light on them, nor any heat; and God shall wipe away all tears from their eyes" (Revelation 7:16–17).

5. Christ appears gloriously above these evils in what He does in His providence in the world as Head and Redeemer of His Church. He appears gloriously above Satan and all his instruments in upholding His Church, even from its first establishment through all the powerful attempts that have been made against it by earth and hell, hereby fulfilling His promise that the gates of hell should never prevail against it (Matthew 16:18).

Christ gloriously triumphed over His enemies in a remarkable success of His gospel soon after His ascension, when many thousands in Jerusalem, and all parts of the world, were so soon turned from darkness unto light, and from the power of Satan unto God, and in causing His Word to go on and prosper, and His Church to increase and prevail against all the opposition of the heathen world when they united all their power to put a stop to it and root it out. So that, in spite of all that the philosophers, wise men, and emperors and princes could do, the gospel in a little time overthrew Satan's old heathenish kingdom in the whole Roman empire (which was then the main part of the world), and so brought about the greatest and most glorious revolution. Instead of one single nation, now the greater part of the nations of the known world had become God's people.

And Christ's exaltation above all evil in His government of the world, in His providence, as the Redeemer of His people, has since gloriously appeared in reviving His Church by the Reformation from popery, after it had for many ages lain in a great measure hidden, and dwelt in a wilderness, under antichristian persecution.

And He will yet far more gloriously triumph over Satan and all his instruments in all the mighty kingdoms that have been set up in opposition to the kingdom of Christ at the time of the fall of antichrist, and the beginning of those glorious times so much spoken of in Scripture prophecy. "Then shall the stone that has been cut out without hands smite all these kingdoms, and break them to pieces; and they shall become like the chaff of the summer threshing-floors, and the wind shall carry them away, that no place should be found for them; and the stone which smote them shall become a great mountain, and fill the whole earth" (Daniel 2:34–35). "Then shall the God of heaven set up a kingdom, which shall never be destroyed; and it shall break in pieces and consume all these kingdoms, and it shall stand forever" (verse 44). "And then the kingdoms of this world shall become the kingdoms of our Lord and of His Christ, and He shall reign forever and ever" (Revelation 11:15). Though great and mighty empires have been set up one after another in the world in opposition to the kingdom of Christ during the succession of so many ages, yet Christ's kingdom shall be the last and the universal kingdom which He has given Him as the heir of the world. Whatever great works Satan has wrought, the final issue and event of all, in the winding up of things in the last ages of the world, shall be the glorious kingdom of Christ through the world—a kingdom of righteousness and holiness, of love and peace, established everywhere. It will be agreeable to the ancient prediction: "I saw in the night visions, and behold, one like the Son of Man came with the clouds of heaven, and came to the Ancient of Days, and they brought Him near before Him. And there was given Him dominion and glory, and a kingdom, that all people, nations, and languages should serve Him; His dominion is an everlasting dominion, which shall not pass away, and His kingdom that which shall not be destroyed. And the kingdom and dominion, and the greatness of the kingdom under the whole heaven, shall be given to the people of the saints of the Most High, whose kingdom is an everlasting kingdom, and all dominions shall serve and obey Him" (Daniel 7:13–14, 27).

Then shall Christ appear gloriously exalted indeed above all evil; and then shall all the saints in earth and heaven gloriously triumph in Him, and sing, "Hallelujah, salvation, and glory, and honor, and power unto the Lord our God; for true and righteous are His judgments; for He hath judged the great whore, which did corrupt the earth with her fornication, and hath avenged the blood of His servants at her hand. Hallelujah: for the Lord God omnipotent reigneth" (Revelation 19:1–2, 6).

6. Christ will appear gloriously above all evil in the consummation of the redemption of His elect Church at the end of the world. Then will be completed the whole work of re-

demption with respect to all whom Christ died for, both in its accomplishment and application, and not till then. And then will Christ's exaltation above all evil be most perfectly and fully manifest. Then shall the conquest and triumph be completed with respect to all of them. Then shall all the devils and all their instruments be brought before Christ to be judged and condemned. And then shall be completed their destruction in their consummate and everlasting misery, when they shall be all cast into the lake of fire, no more to rage and usurp dominion in the world, or have liberty to make opposition against God and Christ. They shall forever be shut up, thenceforward only to suffer. Then shall death be totally destroyed. All the saints shall be delivered everlastingly from it. Even their bodies shall be taken from the power of death by a glorious resurrection.

Then shall all guilt, all sin and corruption, all affliction, and all sighs and tears be utterly and eternally abolished, concerning every one of the elect. They will all be brought to one complete body, to their consummate and immutable glory. And all this as the fruit of Christ's blood, and as an accomplishment of His redemption.

Then all that evil which has so prevailed, and so exalted itself and usurped and raged and reigned, shall be perfectly and forever thrust down and destroyed with respect to all the elect. All will be exalted to a state wherein they will be forever immensely above all these things. "And there shall be no more death, neither sorrow nor crying, neither shall there be any more pain: for the former things are passed away" (Revelation 21:4).

SECTION 3: The subject improved and applied.

1. In this we may see how the glory of the Lord Jesus Christ appears in the work of redemption. It was because the

Father had from eternity a design of exceedingly glorifying His Son that He appointed Him to be the person who should thus triumph over the evil in the world. The work of redemption is the most glorious of all God's works that are made known to us. The glory of God most remarkably shines forth in it. And this is one thing wherein its glory eminently appears, that therein Christ appears so gloriously above Satan and all his instruments; above all guilt, all corruption, all affliction, above death, and above all evil—and more especially because evil has so exalted itself in the world, as we have seen, and exalted itself against Christ in particular.

Satan has ever had a peculiar enmity against the Son of God. Probably his first rebellion, which was his condemnation, was his proudly taking it in disdain when God declared the decree in heaven that His Son, in man's nature, should be the King of heaven, and that all the angels should worship Him. However that was, yet it is certain that his strife has ever been especially against the Son of God. The enmity has always been between the seed of the woman and the serpent. And therefore that war which the devil maintains against God is represented by the devil and his angels fighting against Michael and his angels (Revelation 12:7). This Michael is Christ (Daniel 10:21, 12:1).

God had appointed His Son to be the heir of the world, but the devil has contested this matter with Him, and has strived to set himself up as god of the world. And how exceedingly has the devil exalted himself against Christ! How did he oppose Him as He dwelt among the Jews in His tabernacle and temple! And how did he oppose Him when on earth! And how has he opposed Him since His ascension! What great and mighty works has Satan brought to pass in the world! How many Babels has he built up to heaven in his opposition to the Son of God! How exceedingly proud and haughty has he appeared in his opposition! How have he and his instruments—sin, affliction, and death, of which he is the father—raged against Christ! But yet Christ, in the work of redemption, appears infinitely above them all. In this work He triumphs over them, however they have dealt proudly; and they all appear under His feet. In this the glory of the Son of God, in the work of redemption, remarkably appears.

The beauty of good appears with the greatest advantage when compared with its contrary evil. And the glory of that which is excellent then especially shows itself when it triumphs over its contrary, and appears vastly above it in its greatest height. The glory of Christ, in this glorious exaltation over so great evil that so exalted itself against Him, the more remarkably appears in that He is thus exalted out of so low a state. Though He appeared in the world as a little child, yet how does He triumph over the most gigantic enemies of God and men! He who was "a man of sorrows and acquainted with grief" is a man of war, and triumphed over His enemies in all their power. He who was meek and lowly of heart has triumphed over those proud foes. And He is exalted over them all in that which appears most despicable, even His cross.

2. Here is matter of exceedingly great encouragement for all sinful, miserable creatures in the world of mankind to come to Christ. For let them be as sinful as they will, and ever so miserable, Christ, in the work of redemption, is gloriously exalted above all their sin and misery.

However high their guilt has risen, though mountains have been heaping on mountains all the days of their lives, till the pile appears towering up to heaven, and above the very stars, yet Christ in the work of redemption appears gloriously exalted above all this height. Though they are overwhelmed in a mighty deluge of woe and misery, a deluge that is not only above their heads, but above the heads of the highest mountains, and they do not see how it is possible that they should escape, yet they have no reason to be discouraged from looking to Christ for help. So in the work of redemption, Christ appears gloriously above the deluge of evil. Though they see dreadful corruption in their hearts, though their lusts appear like giants or like the raging waves of the sea, yet they need not despair of help, but may look to Christ, who appears in the work of redemption gloriously above all this corruption.

If they apprehend themselves to be miserable captives of Satan, and find him too strong an adversary for them, and the devil is often tempting and buffeting them and triumphing over them with great cruelty; if it seems to them that the devil has swallowed them up, and has gotten full possession of them, as the whale had of Jonah, yet there is encouragement for them to look again, as Jonah did, towards God's holy temple, and to trust in Christ for deliverance from Satan—that Christ who appears so gloriously exalted above him in the work of redemption.

If they are ready to sink with darkness and sorrows, distress of conscience, or those frowns of God upon them, so that God's waves and billows seem to pass over them, yet they have encouragement enough to look to Christ for deliverance. These waves and billows have before exalted themselves against Christ, and He has proven to be infinitely above them. And if they are afraid of death, if it looks exceedingly terrible as an enemy that would swallow them up, yet let them look to Christ, who has appeared so gloriously above death, and their fears will turn into joy and triumph.

3. What cause have they who have an interest in Christ to glory in their Redeemer! They are often beset with many evils, and many mighty enemies surround them on every side with open mouths ready to devour them; but they need not fear

any of them. They may glory in Christ, the Rock of their salvation, who appears so gloriously above them all. They may triumph over Satan, over this evil world, over guilt, and over death. For as their Redeemer is mighty, and is so exalted above all evil, so shall they also be exalted in Him. They are now, in a sense, so exalted, for nothing can hurt them. Christ carries them as on eagles' wings, high out of the reach of all evils, so that they cannot come near them to do them any real harm. And, in a little time, they shall be carried so out of their reach that these evils shall not be able even to molest them any more forever.

Safety, Fullness, and Sweet Refreshment in Christ

"And a man shall be as a hiding place from the wind, and a covert from the tempest; as rivers of water in a dry place, as the shadow of a great rock in a weary land." Isaiah 32:2

In these words we may observe:
1. The person who is here prophesied of and commended: the Lord Jesus Christ, the King spoken of in the preceding verse who shall reign in righteousness. This King is abundantly prophesied of in the Old Testament, and especially in this prophecy of Isaiah. Glorious predictions were from time to time uttered by the prophets concerning that great King who was to come. There is no subject which is spoken of in so magnificent and exalted a style by the prophets of the Old Testament as the Messiah. They saw His day and rejoiced, and searched diligently, together with the angels, into those things. 1 Peter 1:11–12: "Searching what, or what manner of time, the Spirit of Christ which was in them did signify, when it testified beforehand the sufferings of Christ, and the glory that should follow. Unto whom it was revealed, that not unto themselves, but unto us, they did minister the things, which are now reported unto you by them that have preached the gospel unto you with the Holy Ghost sent down from heaven; which things the angels desire to look into." We are told here that "a man shall be a hiding place from the wind." There is an emphasis in the words that "a man" should be this. If these things had been said of God,

it would not be strange under the Old Testament; for God is frequently called a hiding place for His people, a refuge in time of trouble, a strong rock, and a high tower. But what is so remarkable is that they are said of "a man." But this is a prophecy of the Son of God incarnate.

2. The things here foretold of Him and the commendations given Him. "He shall be a hiding place from the wind, and a covert from the tempest"; that is, He shall be the safety and defense of His people, to which they shall flee for protection in the time of their danger and trouble. To Him they shall flee, as one who is abroad and sees a terrible storm arising, and makes haste to some shelter to secure himself; so that however furious is the tempest, yet he is safe within, and the wind and rain, though they beat never so impetuously upon the roof and walls, are no annoyance to him.

He shall be as "rivers of water in a dry place." This is an allusion to the deserts of Arabia, an exceedingly hot and dry country. One may travel there many days and see no sign of a river, brook, or spring, nothing but a dry and parched wilderness; so that travelers are ready to be consumed with thirst, as the children of Israel were when they were in this wilderness, when they were faint because there was no water. Now when a man finds Jesus Christ, he is like one who has been traveling in those deserts till he is almost consumed with thirst, and who at last finds a river of cool and clear water. And Christ was typified by the river of water that issued out of the rock for the children of Israel in this desert. He is compared to a river because there is such a plenty and fullness in Him.

He is the "shadow of a great rock in a weary land." Allusion is still made to the desert of Arabia. It is not said "as the shadow of a tree," because in some places of that

Safety, Fullness, and Sweet Refreshment in Christ

country, there is nothing but dry sand and rocks for a vast space together, not a tree to be seen; and the sun beats exceedingly hot upon the sands, and all the shade to be found there, where travelers can rest and shelter themselves from the scorching sun, is under some great rock. They who come to Christ find such rest and refreshment as the weary traveler in that hot and desolate country finds under the shadow of a great rock.

We propose to speak to three propositions that are explicatory of the several parts of the text:

1. There is in Christ Jesus abundant foundation of peace and safety for those who are in fear and danger. "A man shall be a hiding place from the wind, a covert from the tempest."

2. There is in Christ provision for the satisfaction, and full contentment, of the needy and thirsty soul. He shall be "as rivers of water in a dry place."

3. There are quiet rest and sweet refreshment in Christ Jesus for him who is weary. He shall be "as the shadow of a great rock in a weary land."

PROPOSITION 1. There is in Christ Jesus an abundant foundation of peace and safety for those who are in fear and danger. The fears and dangers to which men are subject are of two kinds: temporal and eternal. Men are frequently in distress from fear of temporal evils. We live in an evil world, where we are liable to an abundance of sorrows and calamities. A great part of our lives is spent in sorrowing for present or past evils, and in fearing those which are future. What poor, distressed creatures are we when God is pleased to send His judgments among us! If He visits a place with mortal and prevailing sickness, what terror seizes our hearts! If any person is taken sick and trembles for his life, or if our near friends are at the point of death, or in many other dangers, how fearful is our condition! Now there is sufficient foundation for peace and safety to those exercised with such fears and brought into such dangers. But Christ is a refuge in all trouble; there is a foundation for rational support and peace in Him, whatever threatens us. He whose heart is fixed, trusting in Christ, need not be afraid of any evil tidings. As the mountains are round about Jerusalem, so Christ is round about those who fear Him.

But it is the other kind of fear and danger to which we have a principal respect: the fear and danger of God's wrath. The fears of a terrified conscience, the fearful expectation of the dire fruits of sin, and the resentment of an angry God—these are infinitely the most dreadful. If men are in danger of those things, and are not asleep, they will be more terrified than with the fears of any outward evil. Men are in a most deplorable condition, as they are by nature exposed to God's wrath; and if they are sensible how dismal their case is, they will be in dreadful fears and dismal expectations. God is pleased to make some sensible of their true condition. He lets them see the storm that threatens them, how black the clouds are, and how impregnated with thunder, that it is a burning tempest, that they are in danger of being speedily overtaken by it, that they have nothing to shelter themselves from it, and that they are in danger of being taken away by the fierceness of His anger.

It is a fearful condition when one is smitten with a sense of the dreadfulness of God's wrath, when he has his heart impressed with the conviction that the great God is not reconciled to him, that He holds him guilty of these and those sins, and that He is angry enough with him to

Safety, Fullness, and Sweet Refreshment in Christ

condemn him forever. It is dreadful to lie down and rise up; it is dreadful to eat and drink, and to walk about in God's anger from day to day.

One who is in such a case is ready to be afraid of everything; he is afraid of meeting God's wrath wherever he goes. He has no peace in his mind, but there is a dreadful sound in his ears. His mind is afflicted and tossed with tempests, and is not comforted. His courage is ready to fail, and his spirit ready to sink with fear; for how can a poor worm bear the wrath of the great God, and what would he not give for peace of conscience! What would he not give if he could find safety! When such fears exist to a great degree, or continue a long time, they greatly enfeeble the heart, and bring it to a trembling posture and disposition.

Now for such as these there is abundant foundation for peace and safety in Jesus Christ, and this will appear from the following things:

(1) Christ has undertaken to save all such from what they fear, if they come to Him. It is His professional business, the work in which He engaged before the foundation of the world. It is what He always had in His thoughts and intentions. He undertook from everlasting to be the refuge of those who are afraid of God's wrath. His wisdom is such that He would never undertake a work for which He is not sufficient. If there were some in so dreadful a case that He was not able to defend them, or so guilty that it was not fit that He should save them, then He never would have undertaken for them. Those who are in trouble and distressing fear, if they come to Jesus Christ, have this to ease them of their fears: that Christ has promised them that He will protect them; that they come upon His invitation; that Christ has pledged His faith for their security if they will close with Him; and that He is engaged by covenant to God

the Father that He will save those afflicted and distressed souls who come to Him.

Christ, by His own free act, has made Himself the surety of such. He has voluntarily put Himself in their stead; and, if justice has anything against them, He has undertaken to answer for them. By His own act, He has engaged to be responsible for them, so that if they have exposed themselves to God's wrath, and to the stroke of justice, it is not their concern, but His, how to answer or satisfy for what they have done. Let there be never so much wrath that they have deserved, they are as safe as if they never had deserved any, because He has undertaken to stand for them, let it be more or less. If they are in Christ Jesus, the storm does of course light on Him, and not on them; as when we are under a good shelter, the storm that would otherwise come upon our head lights upon the shelter.

(2) He is chosen and appointed of the Father to this work. There needs to be no fear nor jealousy whether the Father will approve of this undertaking of Christ Jesus, whether He will accept Him as a Surety, or whether He will be willing that His wrath should be poured upon His own dear Son instead of us miserable sinners. For there was an agreement with Him concerning it before the world was; it was a thing much upon God's heart, that His Son Jesus Christ should undertake this work, and it was the Father who sent Him into the world. It is as much the act of God the Father as it is of the Son. Therefore, when Christ was near the time of His death, He told the Father that He had finished the work which He gave Him to do. Christ is often called God's elect, or His chosen, because He was chosen by the Father for His work; and God's anointed, for the words "Messiah" and "Christ" signify anointed, because He is by God appointed and fitted for this work.

(3) If we are in Christ Jesus, justice and the law have its course, with respect to our sins, without our hurt. The foundation of the sinner's fear and distress is the justice and the law of God. They are against him, and they are unalterable; they must have their course. Every jot and tittle of the law must be fulfilled; heaven and earth shall be destroyed rather than justice should not take place; there is no possibility of sin's escaping justice.

But yet if the distressed, trembling soul who is afraid of justice would fly to Christ, He would be a safe hiding place. Justice and the threatening of the law will have their course as fully while he is safe and untouched as if he were to be eternally destroyed. Christ bears the stroke of justice, and the curse of the law falls fully upon Him. Christ bears all the vengeance that belongs to the sin that has been committed by him, and there is no need of its being borne twice over. His temporal sufferings, by reason of the infinite dignity of His person, are fully equivalent to the eternal sufferings of a mere creature. And then His sufferings answer for him who flees to Him as well as if they were his own, for indeed they are his own by virtue of the union between Christ and him. Christ has made Himself one with them. He is the head, and they are the members. Therefore, if Christ suffers for the believer, there is no need of his suffering; and what needs he to be afraid? His safety is not only consistent with absolute justice, but it is consistent with the tenor of the law. The law leaves fair room for such a thing as the answering of a surety. If the end of punishment in maintaining the authority of the law and the majesty of the government is fully secured by the sufferings of Christ as his Surety, then the law of God, according to the true and fair interpretation of it, has its course as much in the sufferings of Christ as it would have in his own sufferings. The threatening "thou shalt surely die" is properly fulfilled in the death of Christ, as it is fairly understood. Therefore if those who are afraid will go to Jesus Christ, they need to fear nothing from the threatening of the law. The threatening of the law has nothing to do with them.

(4) Those who come to Christ need not be afraid of God's wrath for their sins; for God's honor will not suffer by their escaping punishment and being made happy. The wounded soul is sensible that he has affronted the majesty of God, and looks upon God as a vindicator of His honor, as a jealous God who will not be mocked, an infinitely great God who will not bear to be affronted, who will not suffer His authority and majesty to be trampled on, who will not bear that His kindness should be abused. A view of God in this light terrifies awakened souls. They think how exceedingly they have sinned, how they have sinned against light, against frequent and long-continued calls and warnings; and how they have slighted mercy, and been guilty of turning the grace of God into lasciviousness, taking encouragement from God's mercy to go on in sin against Him. They fear that God is so affronted at the contempt and slight which they have cast upon Him that He, being careful of His honor, will never forgive them, but will punish them. But if they go to Christ, the honor of God's majesty and authority will not be in the least hurt by their being freed and made happy. For what Christ has done has repaired God's honor to the full. It is a greater honor to God's authority and majesty that, rather than it should be wronged, so glorious a person would suffer what the law required. It is surely a wonderful display of the honor of God's majesty to see an infinite and eternal person dying for its being wronged. And then Christ, by His obedience, by that obedience which He undertook for our

sakes, has honored God abundantly more than the sins of any of us have dishonored Him, however many and however great. How great an honor is it to God's law that so great a person is willing to submit to it and obey it! God hates our sins, but not more than He delights in Christ's obedience which He performed on our account. This is a sweet savor to Him, a savor of rest. God is abundantly compensated, and desires no more. Christ's righteousness is of infinite worthiness and merit.

(5) Christ is a person so dear to the Father that those who are in Christ need not be at all jealous of being accepted upon His account. If Christ is accepted they must of consequence be accepted, for they are in Christ—as members, as parts, as the same. They are the body of Christ, His flesh and His bones. They who are in Christ Jesus are one spirit; and therefore, if God loves Christ Jesus, He must of necessity accept those who are in Him and who are of Him. But Christ is a person exceedingly dear to the Father; the Father's love to the Son is really infinite. God necessarily loves the Son. God could as soon cease to be as cease to love the Son. He is God's elect, in whom His soul delights. He is His beloved Son, in whom He is well pleased. He loved Him before the foundation of the world, and had infinite delight in Him from all eternity. A terrified conscience, therefore, may have rest here, and abundant satisfaction that he is safe in Christ, and that there is not the least danger but that he shall be accepted, and that God will be at peace with him in Christ.

(6) God has given an open testimony that Christ has done and suffered enough, and that He is satisfied with it, by His raising Him from the dead. Christ, when He was in His passion, was in the hands of justice. He was God's prisoner for believers, and it pleased God to bruise Him and

put Him to grief, and to bring Him into a low state; and when He raised Him from the dead, He set Him at liberty, whereby He declared that it was enough. If God was not satisfied, why did He set Christ at liberty so soon? He was in the hands of justice, so why did not God pour out more wrath upon Him, and hold Him in the chains of darkness longer? God raised Him up and opened the prison doors to Him because He desired no more. And now surely there is free admittance for all sinners into God's favor through this risen Savior. There is enough done, and God is satisfied. He has declared it and sealed it by the resurrection of Christ, who is alive and lives for evermore, and is making intercession for poor, distressed souls who come to Him.

(7) Christ has the dispensation of safety and deliverance in His own hands, so that we need not fear but that, if we are united to Him, we may be safe. God has given Him all power in heaven and in earth to give eternal life to whosoever comes to Him. He is made Head over all things to the Church, and the work of salvation is left with Himself. He may save whom He pleases, and defend those who are in Him by His own power. What greater ground of confidence could God have given us than that the Mediator, who died for us and intercedes for us, should have committed to Him the dispensation of the very thing which He died to purchase, and for which He intercedes?

(8) Christ's love, compassion, and gracious disposition are such that we may be sure He is inclined to receive all who come to Him. If He should not do it, He would fail of His own undertaking, and also of His promise to the Father, and to us; and His wisdom and faithfulness will not allow for that. But He is so full of love and kindness that He is disposed to nothing but to receive and defend us if we come to Him. Christ is exceedingly ready to pity us. His

arms are open to receive us. He delights to receive distressed souls who come to Him and to protect them. He would gather them as a hen gathers her chickens under her wings; it is a work that He exceedingly rejoices in because He delights in acts of love, and pity, and mercy.

I shall take occasion from what now has been said to invite those who are afraid of God's wrath to come to Christ Jesus. You are indeed in a dreadful condition. It is dismal to have God's wrath impending over our heads, and not to know how soon it will fall upon us. And you are in some measure sensible that it is a dreadful condition: you are full of fear and trouble, and you know not where to flee for help; your mind is, as it were, tossed with a tempest. But how lamentable is it that you should spend your life in such a condition, when Christ would shelter you as a hen shelters her chickens under her wings, if you were but willing; and that you should live such a fearful, distressed life, when there is so much provision made for your safety in Christ Jesus!

How happy would you be if your hearts were but persuaded to close with Jesus Christ! Then you would be out of all danger: whatever storms and tempests were without, you might rest securely within. You might hear the rushing of the wind, and the thunder roar abroad, while you are safe in this hiding place. Oh, be persuaded to hide yourself in Christ Jesus! What greater assurance of safety can you desire? He has undertaken to defend and save you, if you will come to Him. He looks upon it as His work. He engaged in it before the world was, and He has given His faithful promise which He will not break; and if you will but make your flight there, His life shall be for yours. He will answer for you, and you shall have nothing to do but rest quietly in Him. You may stand still and see what the Lord will do for you. If there is anything to suffer, the suffering is Christ's; you will have nothing to suffer. If there be anything to be done, the doing of it is Christ's; you will have nothing to do but to stand still and behold it.

You will certainly be accepted of the Father if your soul lays hold of Jesus Christ. Christ is chosen and anointed of the Father, and sent forth for this very end: to save those who are in danger and fear. He is greatly beloved of God, even infinitely, and He will accept those who are in Him. Justice and the law will not be against you, if you are in Christ. That threatening, "in the day that thou eatest thou shalt die," in the proper sense of it, will not touch you. The majesty and honor of God are not against you. You need not be afraid that you shall be justified, if you come to Him; there is an act of justification already past and declared for all who come to Christ by the resurrection of Christ. And as soon as ever you come, you are by that declared free.

If you come to Christ, it will be a sure sign that Christ loved you from all eternity, and that He died for you; and you may be sure that, if He died for you, He will not lose the end of His death, for the dispensation of life is committed unto Him.

You need not, therefore, continue in so dangerous a condition; there is help for you. You need not stand out in the storm so long as there is so good a shelter near you, whose doors are open to receive you. Oh, make haste, therefore, unto that Man who is a hiding place from the wind and a covert from the tempest!

Let this truth also cause believers more to prize the Lord Jesus Christ. Consider that it is He, and He only, who defends you from wrath, and that He is a safe defense; your defense is a high tower; your city of refuge is impregnable. There is no rock like your rock. There is none like Christ, "the God of Jeshurun, who rideth upon the heaven in thy help, and in His excellency on the sky; the eternal God is thy refuge, and underneath are everlasting arms" (Deuteronomy 33:26–27). He in whom you trust is a buckler to all who trust in Him. Oh, prize that Savior who keeps your soul in safety, while thousands of others are carried away by the fury of God's anger, and are tossed with raging and burning tempests in hell! Oh, how much better is your case than theirs! And to whom is it owing but to the Lord Jesus Christ? Remember what was once your case, and what it is now, and prize Jesus Christ.

And let those Christians who are in doubts and fears concerning their condition fly anew to Jesus Christ, who is a hiding place from the wind and a covert from the tempest. Most Christians are at times afraid whether they shall not miscarry at last. Such doubtings are always through some want of the exercise of faith, and the best remedy for them is a renewed resort of the soul to this hiding place; the same act which at first gave comfort and peace, will give peace again. They who clearly see the sufficiency of Christ, and the safety of committing themselves to Him to save them from what they fear, will rest in that Christ will defend them. Be directed therefore at such times to do as the psalmist. Psalm 56:3–4: "What time I am afraid, I will trust in Thee. In God I will praise His word, in God I have put my trust. I will not fear what flesh can do unto me."

PROPOSITION 2. There is provision in Christ for the satisfaction and full contentment of the needy and thirsty soul. This is the sense of those words in the text, "as rivers of water in a dry place," in a dry and parched wilderness, where there is a great want of water, and where travelers are ready to be destroyed with thirst, such as was that wilderness in which the children of Israel wandered. This comparison is used elsewhere in the Scriptures. Psalm 63:1: "O God, Thou art my God; early will I seek Thee. My soul thirsteth for Thee, my flesh longeth for Thee in a dry and thirsty land, where no water is." Psalm 143:6: "I stretch forth my hands unto Thee; my soul thirsteth after Thee, as a thirsty land." Those who travel in such a land, who wander in such a wilderness, are in extreme need of water; they are ready to perish for the want of it; and thus they have a great thirst and longing for it.

It is said that Christ is a river of water because there is such a fullness in Him, so plentiful a provision for the satisfaction of the needy and longing soul. When one is extremely thirsty, though, it is not a small draught of water that will satisfy him; yet when he comes to a river, he finds a fullness; there he may drink full draughts. Christ is like a river in that He has a sufficiency not only for one thirsty soul, but by supplying him the fountain is not lessened. There is not the less afforded to those who come afterwards. A thirsty man does not sensibly lessen a river by quenching his thirst.

Christ is like a river in another respect. A river is continually flowing, and there are fresh supplies of water coming from the fountainhead continually, so that a man may live by it, and be supplied with water all his life. So Christ is an ever-flowing fountain. He is continually supplying His people, and the fountain is not spent. They who live upon Christ may have fresh supplies from Him to all eternity; they may have an increase of blessedness that is new, and new still, and which never will come to an end.

In illustrating this second proposition, I shall inquire what it is that the soul of every man naturally and necessarily craves.

First, the soul of every man necessarily craves happi-

Safety, Fullness, and Sweet Refreshment in Christ   93

ness. This is a universal appetite of human nature that is alike in the good and the bad; it is as universal as the very essence of the soul because it necessarily and immediately flows from that essence. It is not only natural to all mankind, but to the angels; it is universal among all reasonable, intelligent beings in heaven, earth, or hell because it flows necessarily from an intelligent nature. There is no rational being, nor can there be any, without a love and desire of happiness. It is impossible that there should be any creature made that should love misery, or not love happiness, since it implies a manifest contradiction; for the very notion of misery is to be in a state that nature abhors, and the notion of happiness is to be in such a state as is most agreeable to nature.

Therefore, this craving of happiness must be insuperable, and what never can be changed; it never can be overcome or in any way abated. Young and old love happiness alike, as do good and bad, wise and unwise—though there is a great variety as to men's ideas of happiness. Some think it is to be found in one thing, and some in another; yet, as to the desire of happiness in general, there is no variety. There are particular appetites that may be restrained, kept under, and conquered, but this general appetite for happiness never can be.

Second, the soul of every man craves a happiness that is equal to the capacity of his nature. The soul of man is like a vessel: the capacity of the soul is as the largeness or contents of the vessel. And therefore, though a man has much pleasure and happiness, yet if the vessel is not full, the craving will not cease. Every creature is restless till it enjoys what is equal to the capacity of its nature. This we may observe in the beasts: when they have that which is suitable to their nature and proportional to their capacity, they are contented. Man is of such a nature that he is capable of an exceedingly great degree of happiness. He is made of a vastly higher nature than the brutes, and therefore he must have vastly higher happiness to satisfy. The pleasures of the outward senses which content the beasts will not content man. He has other faculties of a higher nature that stand in need of something to fill them; if the sense is satiated, yet if the faculties of the soul are not filled, man will be in a craving, restless state.

It is more especially by reason of the faculty of understanding that the soul is capable of so great a happiness, and desires so much. The understanding is an exceedingly extensive faculty; it extends itself beyond the limits of earth, beyond the limits of the creation. As we are capable of understanding immensely more than we do understand, who can tell how far the understanding of men is capable of stretching itself? And as the understanding enlarges, the desire will enlarge with it. It must therefore be an incomprehensible object that will satisfy the soul; it will never be contented with that, and that only, to which it can see an end, it will never be satisfied with that happiness to which it can find a bottom.

A man may seem to take contentment for a little while in a finite object, but after he has had a little experience he finds that he wants something besides. This is very apparent from the experience of this restless, craving world. Everyone is inquiring, "Who will show us any good?"

Men in their fallen state are in very great want of this happiness. They were once in the enjoyment of it, but mankind has sunk to a very low estate. We are naturally poor, destitute creatures. We came naked into the world, and our souls as well as our bodies are in a wretched, miserable condition. We are so far from having food to eat suitable to

Safety, Fullness, and Sweet Refreshment in Christ

our nature that we are greedy after the husks which the swine eat.

The poverty of man in a natural condition appears in his discontented, craving spirit; it shows that the soul is very empty when, like the horse-leech, it cries, "Give, give," and does not say, "It is enough." We are naturally like the prodigal, for we once were rich, but we departed from our father's house, have squandered away our wealth, and have become poor, hungry, famishing wretches.

Men in a natural condition may find something to gratify their senses, but there is nothing to feed the soul; that more noble and more essential part perishes for lack of food. They may fare sumptuously every day; they may pamper their bodies, but the soul cannot be fed from a sumptuous table. They may drink wine in bowls, yet the spiritual part is not refreshed. The superior faculties want to be supplied as well as the inferior. True poverty and true misery consist in the want of those things of which our spiritual part stands in need.

Those sinners who are thoroughly awakened are sensible of their great want. Multitudes of men are not sensible of their miserable, needy condition. There are many who are thus poor, and think themselves rich and increased in goods. Indeed, there are no natural men who have true contentment; they are all restless and crying, "Who will show us any good?" but multitudes are not sensible how exceedingly necessitous is their condition. But the thoroughly awakened soul sees that he is very far from true happiness, that those things which he possesses will never make him happy; that for all his outward possessions he is wretched, miserable, poor, blind, and naked. He becomes sensible of the short continuance and uncertainty of those things, and their insufficiency to satisfy a troubled conscience. He wants something else to give him peace and ease. If you would tell him that he might have a kingdom, it would not quiet him; he desires to have his sins pardoned, and to be at peace with his Judge. He is poor, and he becomes as a beggar; he comes and cries for help. He does not thirst, because he as yet sees where true happiness is to be found, but because he sees that he has it not, and cannot find it. He is without comfort, and does not know where to find it, but he longs for it. Oh, what would he not give if he could find some satisfying peace and comfort!

Such are those hungry, thirsty souls that Christ so often invites to come to Him. Isaiah 55:1-2: "Ho, every one that thirsteth, come ye to the waters, and he that hath no money, come ye, buy and eat; yea, come, buy wine and milk without money and without price. Wherefore do ye spend money for that which is not bread, and your labor for that which satisfieth not? Hearken diligently unto Me, and eat ye that which is good, and let your soul delight itself in fatness." "If any man thirst, let him come unto Me and drink; and he that is athirst, let him come and take of the water of life freely" (John 7:37; Revelation 22:17).

There is in Christ Jesus provision for the full satisfaction and contentment of such as these.

First, the excellency of Christ is such that the discovery of it is exceedingly contenting and satisfying to the soul. The inquiry of the soul is after that which is most excellent. The carnal soul imagines that earthly things are excellent; one thinks riches most excellent, another has the highest esteem of honor, and to another carnal pleasure appears the most excellent; but the soul cannot find contentment in any of these things, because it soon finds an end to their excellency. Worldly men imagine that there is true excellency and true happiness in those things which they are pursuing. They think that if they could but obtain them, they would be happy; and when they obtain them and cannot find happiness, they look for happiness in something else, and are still upon the pursuit.

But Christ Jesus has true excellency, and so great excellency that when they come to see it they look no further, but the mind rests there. It sees a transcendent glory and an ineffable sweetness in Him. It sees that till now it has been pursuing shadows, but that now it has found the substance; that before it had been seeking happiness in the stream, but that now it has found the ocean. The excellency of Christ is an object adequate to the natural cravings of the soul, and is sufficient to fill the capacity. It is an infinite excellency, such a one as the mind desires, in which it can find no bounds; and the more the mind is used to it, the more excellent it appears. Every new discovery makes this beauty appear more ravishing, and the mind sees no end; here is room enough for the mind to go deeper and deeper, and never come to the bottom. The soul is exceedingly ravished when it first looks on this beauty, and it is never weary of it. The mind never has any satiety, but Christ's excellency is always fresh and new, and tends as much to delight, after it has been seen a thousand or ten thousand years, as when it was seen the first moment.

The excellency of Christ is an object suited to the superior faculties of man, suited to entertain the faculty of reason and understanding; and there is nothing so worthy about which the understanding can be employed as this excellency. No other object is so great, noble, and exalted.

This excellency of Jesus Christ is the suitable food of the rational soul. The soul that comes to Christ feeds upon this, and lives upon it. It is that bread which came down from heaven, of which he who eats shall not die; it is angels' food, it is that wine and milk that is given without money and without price. This is that fatness in which the believing soul delights itself. Here the longing soul may be satisfied, and the hungry soul may be filled with goodness. The delight and contentment that is to be found here passes understanding and is unspeakable and full of glory. It is impossible for those who have tasted of this fountain, and know the sweetness of it, ever to forsake it. The soul has found the river of the water of life, and it desires no other drink. It has found the tree of life and it desires no other fruit.

Second, the manifestation of the love of Christ gives the soul abundant contentment. This love of Christ is exceedingly sweet and satisfying; it is better than life because it is the love of a person of such dignity and excellency. The sweetness of His love depends very much upon the greatness of His excellency; so much the more lovely the person, so much the more desirable is his love. How sweet must the love of that person be who is the eternal Son of God, who is of equal dignity with the Father! How great a happiness must it be to be the object of the love of Him who is the Creator of the world, by whom all things consist, who is exalted at God's right hand, and made head over principalities and powers in heavenly places, who has all things put under His feet, who is King of kings and Lord of lords, and is the brightness of the Father's glory! Surely to be beloved by Him is enough to satisfy the soul of a worm of the dust.

This love of Christ is also exceedingly sweet and satisfying from the greatness of it. It is a dying love, such love as never was before seen, and such as no other can parallel.

There have been instances of very great love between one earthly friend and another; there was a surpassing love between David and Jonathan. But there never was any such love as Christ has towards believers. The satisfying nature of this love arises also from the sweet fruits of it. Those precious benefits that Christ bestows upon His people, and those precious promises which He has given them, are the fruit of this love. Joy and hope are the constant streams that flow from this fountain, from the love of Christ.

Third, there is provision for the satisfaction and contentment of the thirsty, longing soul in Christ, as He is the way to the Father; not only from the fullness of excellency and grace which He has in His own person, but as by Him we may come to God, may be reconciled to Him, and may be made happy in His favor and love.

The poverty and want of the soul in its natural state consist in its being separated from God, for God is the riches and the happiness of the creature. But we naturally are alienated from God, and God is alienated from us; our Maker is not at peace with us. But in Christ there is a way for a free communication between God and us; for us to come to God, and for God to communicate Himself to us by His Spirit. John 14:6: "Jesus saith unto him, 'I am the way, and the truth, and the life; no man cometh unto the Father but by Me.' " Ephesians 2:13, 18–19: "But now in Christ Jesus, ye who sometimes were far off are made nigh by the blood of Christ. For through Him we both have access by one Spirit unto the Father. Now, therefore, ye are no more strangers and foreigners, but fellow citizens with the saints, and of the household of God."

Christ, by being thus the way to the Father, is the way to true happiness and contentment. John 10:9: "I am the door: by Me, if any man enter in, he shall be saved, and shall go in and out, and find pasture."

Hence I would take occasion to invite needy, thirsty

souls to come to Jesus. "In the last day, that great day of the feast, Jesus stood and cried, saying, 'If any man thirst, let him come unto Me and drink' " (John 7:37). You who have not yet come to Christ are in a poor, necessitous condition; you are in a parched wilderness, in a dry and thirsty land. And if you are thoroughly awakened, you are sensible that you are in distress and ready to faint for want of something to satisfy your souls. Come to Him who is "as rivers of water in a dry place." There are plenty and fullness in Him. He is like a river that is always flowing; you may live by it forever and never be in want. Come to Him who has such excellency as is sufficient to give full contentment to your soul, who is a person of transcendent glory and ineffable beauty, where you may entertain the view of your soul forever without weariness, and without being cloyed. Accept the offered love of Him who is the only-begotten Son of God, and His elect, in whom His soul delights. Through Christ, come to God the Father, from whom you have departed by sin. He is the way, the truth, and the life. He is the door, by which if any man enters he shall be saved.

PROPOSITION 3. There is quiet rest and sweet refreshment in Christ Jesus for those who are weary. He is "as the shadow of a great rock in a weary land." The comparison that is used in the text is very beautiful and very significative. The dry, barren, and scorched wilderness of Arabia is a very lively representation of the misery that men have brought upon themselves by sin. It is destitute of any inhabitants but lions and tigers and fiery serpents; it is barren and parched, and without any river or spring. It is a land of drought wherein there is seldom any rain, a land exceedingly hot and uncomfortable. The scorching sunbeams that are ready to consume the spirits of travelers are a fit representation of terror of conscience, and the inward

Safety, Fullness, and Sweet Refreshment in Christ

sense of God's displeasure. And there being no other shade in which travelers may rest but only here and there that of a great rock, it is a fit representation of Jesus Christ, who came to redeem us from our misery. Christ is often compared to a rock because He is a sure foundation to builders, and because He is a sure bulwark and defense. They who dwell upon the top of a rock dwell in a most defensible place. We read of those whose habitation is the munitions of rocks. He may also be compared to a rock, as He is everlasting and unchangeable. A great rock remains steadfast, unmoved, and unbroken by winds and storms from age to age; and therefore God chose a rock to be an emblem of Christ in the wilderness when He caused water to issue forth for the children of Israel. The shadow of a great rock is a most fit representation of the refreshment given to weary souls by Jesus Christ.

(1) There is quiet rest and full refreshment in Christ for sinners who are weary and heavy laden with sin. Sin is the most evil and odious thing, as well as the most mischievous and fatal. It is the most mortal poison; it, above all things, hazards life, endangers the soul, exposes it to the loss of all happiness, to the suffering of all misery, and brings the wrath of God. All men have this dreadful evil hanging about them, cleaving fast to the soul, ruling over it, and keeping it in possession and under absolute command. It hangs like a viper to the heart, or rather holds it as a lion does his prey.

But yet there are multitudes who are not sensible of their misery. They are in such a sleep that they are not very unquiet in this condition; it is not very burdensome to them. They are so sottish that they do not know what is their state, and what is likely to become of them. But there are others who have their sense so far restored to them that they feel the pain and see the approaching destruction. Sin lies like a heavy load upon their hearts; it is a load that lies upon them day and night; they cannot lay it down to rest themselves but it continually oppresses them. It is bound fast unto them, and is ready to sink them down; it is a continual labor of heart to support itself under this burden. Thus we read of those "that labor, and are heavy laden." Or rather, it is like the scorching heat in a dry wilderness, where the sun beats and burns all the day long; where they have nothing to defend them; where they can find no shade to refresh themselves. If they lay themselves down to rest, it is like lying down in the hot sands where there is nothing to keep off the heat.

Here it may be proper to inquire who are weary and heavy laden with sin, and in what sense a sinner may be wearied and burdened with sin. Sinners are not wearied with sin from any dislike to it or dislike of it. There is no sinner who is burdened with sin in the sense in which a godly man carries his indwelling sin as his daily and greatest burden, because he loathes it and longs to get rid of it. He would fain be at a great distance from it, and have nothing more to do with it. He is ready to cry out as Paul did, "Oh, wretched man that I am! Who shall deliver me from the body of this death?" The unregenerate man has nothing of this nature, for sin is yet his delight. He dearly loves it. If he is under convictions, his love to sin in general is not mortified. He loves it as well as ever; he hides it still as a sweet morsel under his tongue.

But there is a difference between being wearied and burdened with sin and being weary of sin. Awakened sinners are weary with sin, but not properly weary of it. Therefore, they are only weary of the guilt of sin; the guilt that cleaves to their consciences is that great burden. God has put the sense of feeling into their consciences that were before as seared flesh, and it is guilt that pains them. The filthiness of sin and its evil nature, as it is an offense to a holy, gracious, and glorious God, is not a burden to them. But it is the connection between sin and punishment, between sin and God's wrath, that makes it a burden. Their consciences are heavy laden with guilt, which is an obligation to punishment; they see the threatening and curse of the law joined to their sins, and see that the justice of God and His vengeance are against them. They are burdened with their sins not because there is any odiousness in them, but because there is hell in them. This is the sting of sin, whereby it stings the conscience and distresses and wearies the soul.

The guilt of such and such great sins is upon the soul, and the man sees no way to get rid of it, but he has wearisome days and wearisome nights. It makes him ready sometimes to say as the psalmist did, "O that I had wings like a dove! For then would I fly away and be at rest. Lo, then would I wander far off, and remain in the wilderness. I would hasten my escape from the windy storm and tempest" (Psalm 55:6–8). But when sinners come to Christ, He takes away that which was their burden, or their sin and guilt, that which was so heavy upon their hearts, that so distressed their minds.

First, He takes away the guilt of sin, from which the soul before saw no way possible to be freed, and which, if it was not removed, would lead to eternal destruction. When the sinner comes to Christ, all at once it is taken away, and the soul is left free. It is lightened of its burden; it is delivered from its bondage, and is like a bird escaped from the snare of the fowler. The soul sees in Christ a way to peace with God, and a way by which the law may be answered and justice satisfied, and yet he may escape. This is a wonderful way indeed, but yet a certain and a glorious one. And what rest does it give to the weary soul to see itself thus delivered; that the foundation of its anxieties and fears is wholly removed, and that God's wrath ceases; that it is brought into a state of peace with God, and that there is no more occasion to fear hell, but that it is forever safe!

How refreshing is it to the soul to be at once thus delivered of that which was so much its trouble and terror, and to be eased of that which was so much its burden! This is like coming to a cool shade after one has been traveling in a dry and hot wilderness, and almost fainting under the scorching heat.

And then Christ also takes away sin itself, and mortifies that root of bitterness which is the cause of all the inward tumults and disquietudes that are in the mind, that make it like the troubled sea that cannot rest, and leaves it all calm. When guilt is taken away and sin is mortified, then the foundation of fear, trouble, and pain is removed, and the soul is left in peace and serenity.

Christ puts strength and a principle of new life into the weary soul that comes to Him. The sinner, before he comes to Christ, is as a sick man who is weakened and brought low, and whose nature is consumed by some strong distemper: he is full of pain, and so weak that he cannot walk nor stand. Therefore, Christ is compared to a physician. "But when Jesus heard that, He said unto them, 'They that be whole need not a physician, but they that are sick' " (Mark 2:17). When He comes and speaks the word, He puts a principle of life into him who was before as dead. He gives a principle of spiritual life and the beginning of eternal life. He invigorates the mind with a communication of His own life and strength. He renews the nature and creates it again, and makes the man to be a new creature. So that the fainting, sinking spirits are now revived, and this principle of spiritual life is a continual spring of refreshment, like a well of living water. "Whosoever drinketh of the water that I shall give him, shall never thirst; but the water that I shall give him shall be in him a well of water springing up into everlasting life" (John 4:14).

Christ gives His Spirit that calms the mind, and is like a refreshing breeze of wind. He gives that strength whereby He lifts up the hands that hang down, and strengthens the feeble knees.

Christ gives to those who come to Him such comfort and pleasure as are enough to make them forget all their former labor and travail. A little of true peace, a little of the joys of the manifested love of Christ, and a little of the true and holy hope of eternal life are enough to compensate for all that toil and weariness, and to erase the remembrance of it from the mind. That peace which results from true faith passes understanding, and that joy is joy unspeakable. There is something peculiarly sweet and refreshing in this joy that is not in other joys; and what can more effectually support the mind, or give a more rational ground of rejoicing, than a prospect of eternal glory in the enjoyment of God from God's own promise in Christ? If we come to Christ, we may not only be refreshed by resting in His shadow, but by eating His fruit; these things are the fruits of this tree. "I sat down under his shadow with great delight, and his fruit was sweet to my taste" (Song of Solomon 2:3).

Before proceeding to the next particular of this proposition, I would apply myself to those who are weary, to move them to repose themselves under Christ's shadow. The great trouble of such a state, one would think, should be a motive to you to accept an offer of relief and remedy.

You are weary, and doubtless would be glad to be at rest; but here you are to consider:

First, that there is no remedy but in Jesus Christ; there is nothing else that will give you true quietness. If you could fly into heaven, you would not find it there; if you should take the wings of the morning, and dwell in the uttermost parts of the earth, in some solitary place in the wilderness, you could not fly from your burden. So that if you do not come to Christ, you must either continue still weary and burdened, or, which is worse, you must return to your old dead sleep, to a state of stupidity; and not only so, but you must be everlastingly wearied with God's wrath.

Second, consider that Christ is a remedy at hand. You need not wish for the wings of a dove so that you may fly afar off and be at rest, but Christ is nigh at hand, if you were but sensible of it. Romans 10:6–8: "But the righteousness which is of faith speaketh on this wise, 'Say not in thine heart, "Who shall ascend into heaven?" (that is, to bring Christ down from above) or, "Who shall descend into the deep?" (that is, to bring up Christ again from the dead).' But what saith it? 'The word is nigh thee, even in thy mouth, and in thy heart;' that is, the word of faith which we preach." There is no need of doing any great work to come to this rest; the way is plain to it; it is but going to it; it is but sitting down under Christ's shadow. Christ requires no money to purchase rest of Him. He calls to us to come freely, and for nothing. If we are poor and have no money, we may come. Christ sent out His servants to invite the poor, the maimed, the halting, and the blind. Christ does not want to be hired to accept you, and to give you rest. It is His work as Mediator to give rest to the weary; it is the work that He was anointed for, and in which He delights. "The Spirit of the Lord God is upon Me, because the Lord hath anointed Me to preach good tidings unto the meek; He hath sent Me to bind up the broken-hearted, to proclaim liberty to the captives, and the opening of the prison to them that are bound" (Isaiah 61:1).

Third, Christ is not only a remedy for your weariness and trouble, but He will give you an abundance of the contrary joy and delight. They who come to Christ not only come to a resting place after they have been wandering in a wilderness, but they come to a banqueting house where they may rest, and where they may feast. They may cease from their former troubles and toils, and they may enter upon a course of delights and spiritual joys.

Christ not only delivers from fears of hell and of wrath, but He gives hopes of heaven, and the enjoyment of God's love. He delivers from inward tumults and inward pain, from that guilt of conscience which is as a worm gnawing within, and He gives delight and inward glory. He brings us out of a wilderness of pits, drought, and fiery flying spirits. He brings us into a pleasant land, a land flowing with milk and honey. He delivers us out of prison, lifts us off from the dunghill, sets us among princes, and causes us to inherit the throne of glory.

Wherefore, if anyone is weary, if any is in prison, if any one is in captivity, if anyone is in the wilderness, let him come to the blessed Jesus, who is as the shadow of a great rock in a weary land. Delay not, arise and come away.

(2) There are quiet rest and sweet refreshment in Christ for God's people who are weary. The saints themselves, while they remain in this imperfect state and have so much remains of sin in their hearts, are liable still to many troubles and sorrows, and much weariness, and have often need to resort anew unto Jesus Christ for rest. I shall

mention three cases wherein Christ is a sufficient remedy.

CASE 1. There is rest and sweet refreshment in Christ for those who are wearied with persecutions. It has been the lot of God's Church in this world for the most part to be persecuted. It has had now and then some lucid intervals of peace and outward prosperity, but generally it has been otherwise. This has accorded with the first prophecy concerning Christ: "I will put enmity between thee and the woman, and between thy seed and her seed" (Genesis 3:15). Those two seeds have been at enmity ever since the time of Abel. Satan has borne great malice against the Church of God, as have those who are his seed. Oftentimes God's people have been persecuted to an extreme degree, have been put to the most exquisite torments that wit or art could devise, and thousands have been tormented to death.

But even in such a case there are rest and refreshment to be found in Christ Jesus. When their cruel enemies have given them no rest in this world; when, as oftentimes has been the case, they could not flee, nor in any way avoid the rage of their adversaries (but many of them have been tormented gradually from day to day, that their torments might be lengthened), still rest has been found even then in Christ. It has been often found by experience; the martyrs have often shown plainly that the peace and calm of their minds were undisturbed in the midst of the greatest bodily torment, and have sometimes rejoiced and sung praises upon the rack and in the fire. If Christ is pleased to send forth His Spirit to manifest His love, and speaks friendly to the soul, it will support it even in the greatest outward torment that man can inflict. Christ is the joy of the soul, and if the soul is but rejoiced and filled with divine light, such joy no man can take away; whatever outward misery there is, the spirit will sustain it.

CASE 2. There is in Christ rest for God's people when they are exercised with afflictions. If a person labors under great bodily weakness, or under some disease that causes frequent and strong pains, such things will tire out so feeble a creature as man. It may, to such a one, be a comfort and an effectual support to think that he has a Mediator who knows by experience what pain is; who by His pain has purchased eternal ease and pleasure for him, and who will make his brief sufferings to work out a far more exceeding delight, to be bestowed when he shall rest from his labors and sorrows.

If a person is brought into great straits as to outward subsistence, and poverty brings abundance of difficulties and extremities, yet it may be a supporting, refreshing consideration to such a one to think that he has a compassionate Savior, who, when upon earth, was so poor that He had nowhere to lay His head, and who became poor to make him rich, purchased for him durable riches, and will make his poverty work out an exceeding and eternal weight of glory. If God in His providence calls His people to mourn over lost relations, and if He repeats His stroke and takes away one after another of those who were dear to him, it is a supporting, refreshing consideration to think that Christ has declared that He will be in stead of all relations unto those who trust in Him. They are as His mother, sister, and brother. He has taken them into a very near relation to Himself. And, in every other afflictive providence, it is a great comfort to a believing soul to think that he has an intercessor with God, by whom he can have access with confidence to the throne of grace, and that in Christ we have so many great and precious promises that all things shall work together for good and shall issue in eternal blessedness. God's people, whenever they are scorched by afflictions as by hot sunbeams, may resort to Him who is as a shadow of a great rock, and be effectually sheltered and sweetly refreshed.

CASE 3. There is in Christ quiet rest and sweet refreshment for God's people, when they are wearied with the buffetings of Satan. The devil, that malicious enemy of God and man, does whatever lies in his power to darken, hinder, and tempt God's people, and render their lives uncomfortable. Often he raises needless and groundless scruples, casts in doubts, fills the mind with such fear as is tormenting, and tends to hinder them exceedingly in their Christian course. He often raises mists and clouds of darkness; he stirs up corruption, and thereby fills the mind with concern and anguish, and sometimes wearies the soul, so that they may say as the psalmist: "Many bulls have compassed me: strong bulls of Bashan have beset me round. They gaped upon me with their mouths, as a ravening and a roaring lion" (Psalm 22:12–13).

In such a case if the soul flies to Jesus Christ, he may find rest in Him, for He came into the world to destroy Satan, and to rescue souls out of his hands. He has all things put under His feet, whether they are things in heaven, things on earth, or things in hell; and therefore He can restrain Satan when He pleases. And that He is doubtless ready enough to pity us under such temptations, we may be assured, for He has been tempted and buffeted by Satan as well as we. He is able to succor those who are tempted, and He has promised that He will subdue Satan under His people's feet.

Let God's people therefore, when they are exercised with any of those kinds of weariness, make their resort unto Jesus Christ for refuge and rest.

Reflections

1. We may here see great reason to admire the goodness and grace of God to us in our low estate, that He has so provided for our help and relief. We are, by our own sin against God, plunged into all sorts of evil, but God has provided a remedy for us against every sort of evil. He has left us helpless in no calamity. We, by our sin, have exposed ourselves to wrath, to a vindictive justice; but God has done very great things that we might be saved from that wrath. He has been at infinite cost that the law might be answered without our suffering. We, by our sins, have exposed ourselves to terror of conscience, in expectation of the dreadful storm of God's wrath; but God has provided for us a hiding place from the storm. He bids us enter into His chambers and hide ourselves from indignation. We, by sin, have made ourselves poor, needy creatures; but God has provided for us gold tried in the fire. We, by sin, have made ourselves naked; and when He passed by, He took notice of our want, and has provided us white raiment that we may be clothed. We have made ourselves blind, and God in mercy to us has provided eye-salve that we may see. We have deprived ourselves of all spiritual food; we are like the prodigal son who perished with hunger, and would gladly have filled his belly with husks. God has taken notice of our condition, has provided for us a feast of fat things, and has sent forth His servants to invite the poor, the maimed, the halting, and the blind. We, by sin, have brought ourselves into a dry and thirsty wilderness; but God was merciful, took notice of our condition, and has provided for us rivers of water, water out of the rock. We, by sin, have brought upon ourselves a miserable slavery and bondage; God has made provision for our liberty. We have exposed

ourselves to weariness; God has provided a resting place for us. We, by sin, have exposed ourselves to many outward troubles and afflictions; God has pitied us, and in Christ has provided true comfort for us. We have exposed ourselves to our grand enemy, even Satan, to be tempted and buffeted by him; God has pitied, and has provided for us a Savior and Captain of salvation, who has overcome Satan, and is able to deliver us.

Thus God has, in Christ, provided sufficiently for our help in all kinds of evils. How ought we to bless God for this abundant provision He has made for us, poor and sinful as we were, who were so undeserving and so ungrateful. He made no such provision for the fallen angels, who are left without remedy in all the woes and miseries into which they are plunged.

2. We should admire the love of Christ to men, that He has thus given Himself to be the remedy for all their evil, and a fountain of all good. Christ has given Himself to us, to be all things to us that we need. We want clothing, and Christ not only gives us clothing, but He gives Himself to be our clothing, that we might put Him on. Galatians 3:27: "For as many of you as have been baptized into Christ have put on Christ." Romans 13:14: "But put ye on the Lord Jesus Christ, and make not provision for the flesh, to fulfill the lusts thereof."

We want food, and Christ has given Himself to be our food. He has given His own flesh to be our meat, and His blood to be our drink, to nourish our soul. Thus Christ tells us that He is the bread which came down from heaven, and the bread of life. "I am that bread of life. Your fathers did eat manna in the wilderness, and are dead. This is the bread which cometh down from heaven, that a man may eat thereof, and not die. I am the living bread which came down from heaven; if any man eat of this bread, he shall live forever; and the bread that I will give is My flesh, which I will give for the life of the world" (John 6:48–51). In order for us to eat His flesh, it was necessary that He should be slain, as the sacrifices must be slain before they could be eaten; and such was Christ's love to us that He consented to be slain. He went as a sheep to the slaughter that He might give us His flesh to be food for our poor, famishing souls.

We are in need of a habitation. We, by sin, have, as it were, turned ourselves out of house and home. Christ has given Himself to be the habitation of His people. Psalm 90:1: "Lord, Thou has been our dwelling place in all generations." It is promised to God's people that they should dwell in the temple of God forever, and should go no more out; and we are told that Christ is the temple of the new Jerusalem. Christ gives Himself to His people to be all things to them that they need, and all things that make for their happiness. Colossians 3:11: "There is neither Greek nor Jew, circumcision nor uncircumcision, barbarian, Scythian, bond, nor free; but Christ is all, and in all." And that He might be so, He has refused nothing that is needful to prepare Him to be so.

When it was needful that He should be incarnate, He refused it not, but became man, and appeared in the form of a servant. When it was needful that He should be slain, He refused it not, but gave Himself *for* us, and gave Himself *to* us upon the cross.

Here is love for us to admire, for us to praise, and for us to rejoice in, with joy that is full of glory forever.

Jesus Christ the Same Yesterday, Today, and Forever
(Hebrews 13:8)

The exhortation which the Apostle gives the Hebrew Christians in the verse preceding this is to remember and follow the good instructions and examples of their ministers: "Remember them who have the rule over you, who have spoken unto you the word of God; whose faith follow, considering the end of their conversation." The last part of this exhortation is to follow their faith. By "following their faith," the Apostle seems to intend adhering to the Christian faith, those wholesome doctrines which their pastors taught them, and not depart from them, as many in that day had done, to heretical tenets. And the enforcement of the doctrine is in these words: "Considering the end of their conversation, Jesus Christ the same yesterday, today, and forever." Christ is the end of their conversation. He is the end of their conversation in their office, the end of the doctrines which they taught, and the end of all their administrations and labors in all their work. And as He was so, they ought to follow their faith, or cleave steadfastly to the doctrines they had taught them, and not depart to other doctrines; for Jesus Christ is the same, yesterday, today, and forever.

If they still professed to be Christians, or the followers of Jesus Christ, they should still cleave to the same doctrines that they were taught in their first conversion. They should still follow the faith of those who had first indoctrinated them in

Christianity; for Jesus Christ is the same now as He was then, and therefore Christianity is obviously the same thing. It is not one thing now and another when they were first converted, or even like any other thing than it always had been. Surely therefore, when Christ and Christianity were thus unchangeable, he would therefore have them not be fickle and changeable in their faith, not depart from their former faith, nor be carried about with divers and strange doctrines, as follows in the next verse.

When it is said that Christ is the same yesterday, today, and forever, by "yesterday" is meant all time past; by "today" the time present; and by "forever" all that is future, from the present time to eternity.

DOCTRINE: Jesus Christ is the same now that He ever has been and ever will be.

Christ is thus unchangeable in two respects.

1. In His divine nature. As Christ is one of the persons of the Trinity, He is God, and so has the divine nature, or the Godhead, dwelling in Him; and all the divine attributes belong to Him, of which immutability or unchangeableness is one. Christ, in His human nature, was not absolutely unchangeable, though His human nature, by reason of its union with the divine, was not liable to those changes to which it was liable as a mere creature. For instance, it was indestructible and imperishable. Having the divine nature to uphold it, it was not liable to fall and commit sin, as Adam and the fallen angels did; but yet the human nature of Christ, when He was upon earth, was subject to many changes. It had a beginning; it was conceived in the womb of the Virgin; it was in a state of infancy, and afterwards changed from that state to a state of manhood, and this was attended not only with a change in His body, by His increasing in stature, but also in His mind; for we read that He not only increased in stature, but also in

wisdom (Luke 2:52).

The human nature of Christ was subject to sorrowful changes, though not to sinful ones. He suffered hunger, thirst, and cold; and at last He suffered dreadful changes by having His body tortured and destroyed, and His soul poured out unto death. Afterwards He became subject to a glorious change at His resurrection and ascension. And that His human nature was not liable to sinful changes, as Adam's or the angels', was not owing to anything in His human nature, but to its relation to the divine nature which upheld it. But the divine nature of Christ is absolutely unchangeable, and not liable to the least alteration or variation in any respect. It is the same now as it was before the world was created. It was the same after Christ's incarnation as before, when Christ was born in a stable and laid in a manger, and underwent many changes on earth, and at last suffered that dreadful agony in the garden, and suffered on the cross—it made no real alteration in the divine nature. And afterwards, when Christ was glorified, and sat on the right hand of the Majesty on high, it made no alteration in His divine nature.

2. Christ is unchangeable in His office. He is unchangeable as the Mediator and Savior of His church and people. That unchangeableness of Christ in His office of Mediator appears in several things:

(1) This office never ceases in order to give place to any other to come in His stead. Christ is the only Mediator between God and man who ever has been or ever shall be. He is an everlasting Savior. There have been many typical mediators who have continued but a little while and then have passed away, and others have come in their place; but the great antitype continues forever. There have been prophets who have been raised up, but these have died and others have succeeded them. Moses was not suffered to continue by

reason of death, and the dispensation which he introduced was abolished to give place to another which Christ should introduce. Moses gives place to Christ, but Christ never gives place to any other.

John the Baptist was a great prophet. He was Christ's forerunner; like the morning star, the forerunner of the sun, he shone bright for a little while, but his ministry by degrees ceased and gave way to the ministry of Christ, as the morning star by little and little goes out as the sun rises. John the Baptist said, "He must increase, but I must decrease" (John 3:30). But Christ's ministry never ceases. So the ancient legal priests had but a changeable and short-lived priesthood. Aaron died and his son Eleazar succeeded him. And so there were many priests, one after another, but Christ continues as a priest forever (Hebrews 7:23–24). There were truly many priests, and they were not suffered to continue by reason of death; but Christ, because He continues forever, has an unchangeable priesthood. These legal priests succeeded one another by inheritance—the father died and the son succeeded him, and then he died and his son succeeded him—but it is observed that Christ, in His priesthood, "is without father and without mother, without descent." He had no ancestor who went before Him in His priesthood, or any posterity that should succeed Him in it. In that respect, Melchizedek is a type of Christ, of whom the Scripture gives an account that he was a priest, but seems not to have been a priest by inheritance, as the sons of Aaron were. Hebrews 7:3: "Without father, and without mother, and without descent, having neither beginning of days, nor end of life, but made like unto the Son of God, he abideth a priest continually." And therefore it is said of Christ in Psalm 110:4: "The Lord hath sworn and will not repent. 'Thou art a priest forever after the order of Melchizedek.' "

Those things that pertain to Christ's priesthood are everlasting. The tabernacle at which the priests of old officiated was a tabernacle that men pitched, and therefore a tabernacle that was taken down. It was the holy of holies of old; but Christ is a minister of the true tabernacle and the true sanctuary, which the Lord has built and not man (Hebrews 8:2). The holy of holies He entered into was heaven. He is priest in a tabernacle which shall never be taken down, and in a temple that shall never be demolished. So the altar on which He offers incense, the priestly garments or robes in which He officiates, are not of a corruptible nature.

And so Christ is everlasting with reference to His kingly office. David and Solomon were great kings, and eminent types of Christ; but death put an end to their kingdom and greatness. Earthly monarchies that ever have been, those that have ruled over the bigger part of the known world, as particularly the Grecian and Roman monarchies, have come to an end. But Christ's is an everlasting kingdom. His throne is forever and ever. Hebrews 1:8: "Thy throne, O God, is forever and ever; a scepter of righteousness is the scepter of Thy kingdom." Though all other kingdoms shall be demolished, Christ's kingdom shall stand forever (Daniel 7:13–14).

(2) Christ is at all times equally sufficient for the office He has undertaken. He undertook the office from eternity, and He was sufficient for it from eternity. He has been in the exercise of His office from the fall of man, and remains equally sufficient throughout all ages. His power and His wisdom, His love, His excellency and worthiness, are at all times equally sufficient for the salvation of sinners, and for the upholding and glorifying of believers. He is forever able to save because He lives forever. His life is an endless and unchangeable life. He is made not after the law of a carnal commandment, but after the power of an endless life (Hebrews 7:16).

He is at all times equally accepted as a Mediator in the sight of the Father, who is ever well pleased in Him. He is always equally worthy and lovely in His eyes. He is daily His delight, rejoicing always before Him. The sacrifice that He has offered, and the righteousness that He has performed, are at all times equally sufficient. His blood is as sufficient to cleanse away sin now as when it was warm from His wounds.

    (3) He is now, and ever will be, the same that He ever has been in the disposition and will which He exercises in His office. He is not changeable in His disposition, as men are who are called to any office or business which causes them to appear and act very differently in their offices at some times from what they do at others. But Jesus Christ is in this respect the same yesterday, today, and forever. He is ever disposed to execute His office in a holy manner. He ever has been, still is, and ever will be disposed to execute it so as to glorify His Father, to discountenance sin, and to encourage holiness. He ever exercised the same grace and mercy in His office. He undertook the office of a Mediator from eternity with delight. He then delighted in the thought of saving sinners, and He still delights in it. He never has altered from the disposition to accomplish it. When man actually fell and became a rebel and an enemy, an enemy to his Father and himself, still it was His delight to do the part of a Mediator for him. And when He came into the world, and came to His last agony; when the bitter cup that He was to drink was set before Him, and He had an extraordinary view of it, so that the sight of it made "His soul exceedingly sorrowful even unto death" (Matthew 26:38), and caused Him to "sweat as it were great drops of blood" (Luke 22:44), still He retained His disposition to do the part of a Mediator for sinners, and delighted in the thoughts of it. So even when He was enduring the cross, the salvation of sinners was a joy set before Him (Hebrews 12:2).

And He never alters from His readiness to receive and embrace all who in faith come to Him. He is always equally willing to receive such. His love is unchangeable. He loved from eternity. Jeremiah 31:3: "He loved with an everlasting love"; and it will be to eternity. John 13:1: "Having loved His own, He loved them unto the end."

(4) Christ is the same yesterday, today, and forever as to the end which He aims at in His office. His supreme end in it is the glory of God, particularly in vindicating the honor of His majesty, justice, and holiness, and the honor of His holy law. For this end did He undertake to stand as a Mediator between God and man, and to suffer for men: that the honor of God's justice, majesty, and law might be vindicated in His sufferings. He also undertook the office to glorify the free grace of God; and His special end in His undertaking was the salvation and happiness of the elect. These two ends He has in His eye in all parts of the work of His office; and these two ends He unchangeably aims at. These He sought in entering into covenant with the Father from eternity. These He has sought from the beginning of the world to this time, and these He ever will seek. He does not sometimes pursue one end and then alter His mind and pursue another, but He ever pursues the same ends.

(5) Christ ever acts by the same rules in the execution of His mediatorial office. The rules that Christ acts by in the execution of His office are contained in a twofold covenant:

[1] The covenant of redemption, or the eternal covenant that was between the Father and Son, wherein Christ undertook to stand as Mediator with fallen man, and was appointed thereto of the Father. In that covenant, all things concerning Christ's execution of His mediatorial office were agreed between Christ and His Father, and established by them. And this covenant or eternal agreement is the high-

est rule that Christ acts by in His office; it is a rule that He never in the least departs from. He never does anything more or less than is contained in that eternal covenant. Christ does the work that God gave Him to do in that covenant, and no other. He saves those, and those only, whom the Father gave Him in that covenant to save; and He brings them to such a degree of happiness as was therein agreed. To this rule Christ is unchangeable in this regard; it stands good with Christ in every article of it, yesterday, today, and forever.

[2] Another covenant that Christ has regard to in the execution of His mediatorial office is that covenant of grace which God established with man. Though indeed this is less properly the rule by which Christ acts as Mediator than the covenant of redemption, yet it may be called a rule. God, as it were, makes His promise, which He makes to His creatures, His rule to act by; all His actions are in an exact conformity to His promise, and He never departs in the least degree from them, as is the case with men with regard to what they make the rule of their actions. Yet it is not a rule to God in the same sense as a rule is to a created agent, which must be considered as something antecedent to the purposes of the agent, and that by which his purposes are regulated. But God's promises are consequent on His purposes, and are no other than the expressions of them. And the covenant of grace is not essentially different from the covenant of redemption: it is but an expression of it. It is only that covenant of redemption partly revealed to mankind for their encouragement, faith, and comfort. And therefore the fact that Christ never departs from the covenant of redemption infers that He will never depart from the covenant of grace; for all that was promised to men in the covenant of grace was agreed on between the Father and the Son in the covenant of redemption. However, there is one thing wherein Christ's un-

changeableness in His office appears: He never departs from the promises that He has made to man. There is the same covenant of grace in all ages of the world. The covenant is not essentially different now from what it was under the Old Testament, and even before the flood; and it always will remain the same. It is therefore called an "everlasting covenant" in Isaiah 55:3.

And as Christ does not alter His covenant, so He unchangeably fulfills it. He never departs in the least jot or tittle. Though He has given exceedingly great and precious promises to those who believe in Him, He ever fulfills them all. Heaven and earth shall sooner pass away than one jot or one tittle of His promises shall fail, till all is fulfilled. It is especially on account of His unchangeableness with respect to His promises that He calls Himself "I am that I am," and is called "Jehovah" (Exodus 3:14 and 6:3). Christ revealed Himself to the children of Israel in their Egyptian bondage by this name to encourage the descendants of Abraham, Isaac, and Jacob.

(6) He is, in many respects, unchangeable in the acts which He exercises in His office. He is unchangeable in His acceptance of those who believe in Him, and never will reject them. He is unchangeable in His complacency and delight in them. He is unchangeable in His intercession for His church and people. He ever lives to make intercession (Hebrews 7:25). His intercession before God in heaven is a continual intercession. It is a constant presentation of His will before the Father for the salvation and happiness of those who are His by virtue of His blood. And as Christ is unchangeable in His intercession, so He is unchangeable in upholding and preserving those who are His, and ordering all things for their good, until they are brought to His heavenly glory. He is constant and unchangeable in taking care of them in all respects, and

will hereafter receive them to a constant and unchangeable enjoyment of Himself.

Application

1. We learn from the truth taught in the text how fit Christ was to be appointed as the Surety of fallen man. Adam, the first surety of mankind, failed in his work because he was a mere creature, and so a mutable being. Though he had so great a trust committed to him, such as the care of the eternal welfare of all his posterity, yet, not being unchangeable, he failed and transgressed God's holy covenant. He was led aside and drawn away by the subtle temptation of the devil. Being a changeable being, his subtle adversary found means to turn him aside and so he fell, and all his posterity fell with him. It appeared, therefore, that we stood in need of a surety who was unchangeable and could not fail in his work. Christ, whom God appointed to this work to be to us a second Adam, is such a one who is the same yesterday, today, and forever, and therefore was not liable to fail in His undertaking. He was sufficient to be depended on as one who would certainly stand all trials and go through all difficulties until He had finished the work that He had undertaken, and actually wrought out eternal redemption for us.

2. This truth may be well applied to the awakening of those who profess to be Christians, and this on several accounts. You may be hence assured that Christ will fulfill the threatenings that He has pronounced against unbelievers. There are many awful threatenings which Christ has pronounced against wicked men. Christ has threatened woe to this wicked world, and has declared concerning all who do

not believe that they shall be damned. This is that which Christ gave in a charge to His disciples before His ascension, when He sent them forth to preach and teach all nations. Mark 16:15–16: "Go ye into all the world, and preach the gospel to every creature. He that believeth shall be saved, and he that believeth not shall be damned." So Christ declared that "every tree that bringeth not forth good fruit shall be hewn down, and cast into the fire" (Matthew 7:19). And He has especially threatened an awful punishment to gospel sinners. He has declared that every branch in Him that bears not fruit shall be cut off, cast forth, and gathered up and burnt. However wicked men and false Christians may dwell among the godly, as tares grow among wheat, yet when the harvest comes, and the wheat is gathered into the barn, the tares shall be gathered into bundles and burned (Matthew 13:30). And in the explication of the parable He says that at the day of judgment "the Son of Man shall send forth His angels, and they shall gather out of His kingdom all things that offend, and them that do iniquity, and shall cast them into a furnace of fire, where shall be wailing and gnashing of teeth" (verses 41–42). So He declares in Matthew 7:21–23, concerning those outwardly visible Christians who say to Him, "Lord, Lord," and who do not do the will of His Father which is in heaven, that He will hereafter profess unto them that He never knew them, and that He will say unto them, "Depart from Me, ye that work iniquity." He declares that those who build their house on the sand shall fall, and that great shall be their fall; and that such as these shall see many coming from the east, west, north, and south, and sitting down with Abraham, and Isaac, and Jacob, in the kingdom of God, and themselves thrust out.

He teaches in His parables that unprofitable servants, and those who as professing Christians come to the gospel feast without the wedding garment, shall be bound hand and foot and cast into outer darkness, where shall be weeping and gnashing of teeth. He often pronounces woe on hypocrites, and threatens concerning such as begin a life of religion and do not finish, and are not thorough and persevering in it, that they shall come to shame; that those who are foolish virgins, who take their lamps and take no oil with them, shall at last be shut from the marriage when others enter in with the bridegroom; and that when they come to the door they shall find it shut, and shall cry, "Lord, Lord, open to us," in vain. He declares that, at the day of judgment, He shall separate the righteous from the wicked, as a shepherd divides his sheep from the goats, setting the righteous on the right hand and the wicked on the left hand. He shall say to the wicked, "Depart, accursed, into everlasting fire, prepared for the devil and his angels"; and the wicked shall go away into everlasting punishment.

Particularly He has threatened concerning those who have not a spirit of self-denial, who do not cut off a right hand or a right foot, nor pluck out a right eye, that they shall go with two hands, two feet, or two eyes into hell-fire; into the fire that never shall be quenched, "where the worm dieth not, and the fire is not quenched" (Mark 9:44). And those who have not a spirit to sell all for His sake, and who do not in comparison to Him hate father, mother, wife, and every earthly relative and earthly possession, shall not be acknowledged of Him as His disciples. And concerning those who are ashamed of religion before men, of them will He be ashamed before His Father and before the angels.

Concerning those who are of a vengeful spirit and not a spirit of forgiveness, they shall not be forgiven; and concerning all who are of a malicious spirit and not a spirit of Christian love and meekness, who are of an angry, wrathful, and scornful disposition, who say to their brother, "Raca," or "Thou fool"—they shall be in danger of everlasting punishment proportioned to the heinousness of their crimes. And concerning worldly-minded men He has declared that it is impossible for those who trust in riches to enter into the kingdom of God. Concerning such He has said, "Woe unto you that are rich, for ye have received your consolation; and woe unto you that are full, for ye shall hunger.'"

Concerning such as are addicted to carnal mirth and jollity, He says, "Woe unto you that laugh now, for ye shall mourn and weep." And He has abundantly declared concerning gospel sinners that their punishment shall be far more dreadful than that of the worst of the heathen; that it shall be more tolerable even for Sodom and Gomorrah in the day of judgment than for them. He has declared that those who are once cast into hell shall in no wise come out thence until they have paid the uttermost farthing.

Such things as these Christ threatened against the ungodly when He was here upon earth. And by the doctrine of the text, you learn that He now is and ever will be the same as He was then. He has not at all altered, no, nor ever will; but these dreadful things that He has threatened He will surely fulfill. Christ was no more disposed to threaten than to fulfill His threatenings. Christ is as holy, and His nature and will are as averse to sin now as ever they were; and He is as strictly just now as He was then.

Therefore, let no Christ-less person flatter himself that, continuing such, He shall by any means escape punishment. Christ's threatenings are the threatenings of one who is the same yesterday, today, and forever; and what He has threatened with His mouth He will fulfill with His hands. When Christ appears at the day of judgment, and you shall stand at His bar to be judged, you will find Him to be in judging just what He was, and just what you find Him in your Bibles to be, in threatening.

USE OF REPROOF:
1. The truth of the text may be applied to those who have been heretofore under awakenings, but have now become senseless and careless. This doctrine shows your folly. You act as if Christ were altered, as though He were not now so dreadful a Judge, and His displeasure not so much to be feared as heretofore. Time was when you were afraid of the displeasure and wrath of Christ. You were afraid of the dreadful sentence from His mouth, "Depart, ye cursed, into everlasting fire." And why is it so much otherwise with you now? Is not the wrath of this Judge as much to be dreaded now as ever it was? Time was when those threatenings that Christ has pronounced against sinners were terrible things to you; and why do you make so light of them now? Has your great Judge grown weaker than He was, and less able to fulfill His threatenings? Are you less in His hands than you were, or do you imagine that Christ has become more reconciled to sin, and has not such a disposition to execute vengeance for it as He had?

Time was when you seemed to feel yourself to be in lamentable circumstances: that you had no interest in Christ, nor had a great mind to get an interest in Him. You sought it, prayed to God daily for it, took considerable pains, and went and asked others what you should do to obtain an interest in Christ. Why is it that you are so much more careless about it now? Is Christ altered? Is an interest in Him less valuable or less necessary now than it was then? Was acceptance with Him worth earnestly seeking, praying, and striving for then, and is it good for nothing now? Did you stand in great need of it then, and can you do well enough without it now?

Time was when you seemed to be much concerned about your having been guilty of so much sin against God and Christ, and, it may be, wept about it in your prayers. But now you are not concerned about it. The thought of your having so often and so greatly offended Him does not so much trouble you, but you can be easy and quiet, and have your heart taken up about one vanity or another, without being greatly disturbed with the thoughts of your sins. Then you used to be careful to avoid sin: you were watchful to avoid those things that were forbidden in God's holy Word; you were careful that you did not sin by profaning the sabbath, by unsuitably spending the time in God's house, or by neglecting the duties of reading and prayer. You were careful of your behavior among men, lest you should transgress. If you suspected anything to be sinful then, you dared not do it.

But now there is no such care upon your spirit; there is no such watch maintained; you have no such guard upon you. But when you are tempted to do or omit anything, there is not a thought coming with weight upon your heart, "Is this sinful or not?" or "Is this contrary to the mind and will of God or not?" You do not dwell long on such kind of thoughts as these; you are grown very bold and live in neglects and practices that are sinful, and you have light enough to know them to be so—as if you thought that Christ's disposition with respect to sin was altered, and that He was less an enemy to sin now than He was then. Instead of being less an enemy to sin than you then thought He was, and instead of being a less dreadful Judge of ungodly men than you then imagined, or had a sense of in your heart, He is a thousand times more so. For then, when you were most awakened and convinced, you conceived but very little of what is in reality; you apprehended very imperfectly the enmity of Christ's nature against sin and the dreadfulness of His wrath against the ungodly. It was but a

Jesus Christ The Same Yesterday, Today, and Forever

little sense you had of it. His wrath is infinitely more dreadful than ever you have yet had any conception of.

And though Christ is unchangeable, yet you are not. You are changed for the worse since the time when you were awakened. Christ is equally an enemy of sin, and you have become more sinful than you then were. Christ's wrath is in itself equally dreadful as it then was, but you have far more reason to dread it than you had then, for you are in much greater danger of it. And if you do not repent, you are much nearer to the exception of it. And not only so, but you are now exposed to much more of that wrath. Christ's wrath hung over your head then, and so it does now, but with this difference: that now much more of that wrath hangs over you than did then. You hung over the pit of hell then, and so you do now; but with this difference: that you have ever since been kindling and enraging the flames of that fiery gulf over which you hang, so that they are vastly fiercer than they were then. The moth of time has been nibbling at that slender thread ever since, and has much more nearly gnawed it off than it had then. Your heart is far more hardened than it was; the devil has faster hold of you, and the way to escape is more blocked up. Your case, upon many accounts, is inexpressibly more doleful, however much more careless and unconcerned you are about your own circumstances.

2. This doctrine reproves all who have entered into the bonds of the Christian covenant, and have proven false to it. If Christ is the same yesterday, today, and forever, and is always the same towards us in fulfilling as He is in promising, then surely we ought to be so towards Him. If He never breaks covenant with His people, then they are greatly to be reproved who are false and treacherous in their dealings with Him. Therefore this reproves a covenant people who depart from Christ and break covenant with Him, as we in this land

have done, having greatly revolted and degenerated both from the pure profession and religious practice of the first times of the country. Though Christ and His doctrine, and the religion that He taught, are always the same, yet this country has great multitudes in it who are driven to and fro by every wind of doctrine, and have now, for a long time, been exceedingly corrupted by the prevalence of many evil customs and practices.

And by this doctrine is every particular person reproved who does not take care to keep covenant with Christ. We are in general under the solemn bonds of our baptismal covenant; and that covenant that was sealed in our baptism most of us have explicitly owned and expressly and solemnly promised to walk in, in a way of obedience to all the commands of God, as long as we live. We have, time after time, in the most solemn manner, sealed this covenant anew by taking the body and blood of Christ upon it at the Lord's Supper. They bring dreadful guilt on themselves who are not careful to fulfill such vows. Those who have solemnly vowed to obey Christ in all His commandments as long as they live, and have sealed these vows by eating and drinking at the Lord's Supper with far greater solemnity than if they sealed it with as many solemn oaths, yet who live in ways of sin, in the neglect of several commanded duties, and in the commission of forbidden sin, or at least do not make it the care of their lives strictly to keep Christ's commands—surely such persons render themselves very guilty.

3. This doctrine reproves those who have been seemingly pious, and have fallen away to ways of sin. Who these persons are, their own consciences are better able to judge than those who are about them. There are many here present who in times past have been seemingly pious; and let everyone inquire at the mouth of his own conscience whether his seem-

ing piety holds on, whether it has not come to an end. If you find reason, by a serious and strict examination, to conclude that you are one of them, consider how vile is your treatment of Him who is the same yesterday, today, and forever, and who never is false to any to whom He once manifests His favor. How greatly does God complain of short-lived religion in the Scriptures! Hosea 6:4: "O Ephraim, what shall I do unto thee? O Judah, what shall I do unto thee? for your goodness is as a morning cloud, and as the early dew it goeth away." Psalm 78:56–57: "They tempted and provoked the most high God, and kept not His testimonies, but turned back and dealt unfaithfully like their fathers; they were turned aside like a deceitful bow."

4. Hereby the truly godly are greatly to be reproved for their declension. There are many such here, as I charitably hope, and many of them I fear have been guilty of great declension in religion. Formerly they were lively and animated in religion; now they are dull and indifferent. Formerly their hearts went up on high after God, but now after the world; they carried themselves for a while very exemplarily, but have since behaved in such a manner as to wound religion. Why will you be guilty of such a departure from your Redeemer, who changes not with regard to you? His love He formerly manifested towards you, but it does not change; it has ever held up to the same height. His faithfulness never has failed you; why, then, does your love so languish towards Him, and why are you so unfaithful to Him? He keeps up the same care and watchfulness towards you, to preserve you, to provide for you, to defend you from your enemies; and why will you suffer your care and strictness to serve and please Christ, and honor Him, to fail in any measure?

When you were first converted, your heart seemed to be wrapped up in love to Christ, and delight in Him and His praises. You were then continually meditating on Christ and the things of Christ, and your meditations on Him were sweet. You were then much in speaking of those things, and you delighted to speak of them. And why is it so much otherwise with you now? Is Christ less excellent than He was then? Is He less worthy of your love?

5. This doctrine affords matter of reproof to us of this town, for our declining is much from what we have lately been. That we have exceedingly declined in religion is most manifest, and what all confess. A little while ago Christ was the great object of regard among us. The hearts of the people in general were greatly engaged about Christ, as though Christ had been all and the world nothing. There was then a great deal of conversation among all sorts of persons, and in all companies, of Christ. They who thought they had no interest in Christ were full of concern how to obtain an interest in Him; and they were almost ready to neglect their worldly concerns, as though Christ was all they needed. And with regard to those who thought they had obtained an interest in Christ, their thoughts and their conversation seemed also to be very much taken up about Christ. They were much engaged in talking of the excellency of Christ, and seemed to be full of the grace and dying love of Christ. And one and another of you expressed the strong sense you had of one perfection and excellency and another of Christ, and of the glory of the works that He has done and the sweetness of the words that He speaks.

The town seemed to be full of the praises of Christ. You expressed to one another how you earnestly longed to praise Him and bless His name forever and ever, and how you desired that others should help you to praise Him. The benefits procured by Christ were then greatly valued in the town, and both Christ and His benefits were then precious among us.

Multitudes seemed to be concerned as to what they should do for the honor of Christ, how they should live to His glory and do something for the advancement of His kingdom in the world. But now, how much otherwise is it! How little is Christ set by in comparison to what He has been! How much is He neglected! How much has He dropped out of people's common discourse and conversation! How have many of you left off earnestly following Christ to pursue after the world: one to pursue after riches, another to be engrossed by amusement and diversion, another by fine clothes and gay apparel; and all sorts, young and old, have gone their way wandering in a great measure from Christ—as though Christ was not as excellent now as He was then; as though His grace and dying love were not as wonderful now as they were then; as though Christ was not now as much preferable to the world, as worthy to be loved, to be praised, to be thought of and talked of; and as though He was not as worthy that we should be concerned to honor Him, and live to His praise, as ever He was. If Christ is as much altered as the town is altered, He is altered very much indeed! Are we so foolish as to think that He, who is the same yesterday, today, and forever, is so much altered from what He was three years ago?

USE OF ENCOURAGEMENT:
1. The truth taught in the text may be applied by way of encouragement to sinners whose minds are burdened and exercised with concern about the state of their souls, to come to Christ and put their trust in Him for salvation. If Christ is now and ever will be the same as He ever was, then here is great encouragement for you to come to Him, as will appear by considering two things:

(1) How Christ has invited you to come to Him, with promises that He will accept you if you do so. Christ in His

Word often invites those who are in your circumstances, whether we consider your circumstances as a lost sinner or as a sinner under anxiety and concern about your condition. If we consider your circumstances merely as a lost sinner, Christ invites you; for He is often inviting and calling on sinners to come to Him. Proverbs 8:4: "Unto you, O men, I call, and my voice is to the sons of men." And Proverbs 9:4–5: "Whoso is simple, let him turn in hither; and ye that want understanding, come, eat of My bread, and drink of the wine that I have mingled." Revelation 3:20: "Behold, I stand at the door and knock." Revelation 22:17: "The Spirit and the bride say, 'Come.'" Or if we consider your circumstances as a sinner burdened in your soul with concern about your condition, such are especially invited by Christ. Matthew 11:28: "Come unto Me, all ye that labor and are heavy laden, and I will give you rest." Isaiah 55:1: "Ho, every one that thirsteth, come ye to the waters." John 7:37: "If any man thirst, let him come unto Me and drink." That Christ is the same yesterday, today, and forever shows what a joint encouragement these invitations are for you to come to Christ in two ways:

First, it shows that as Christ invited such sinners when these invitations were spoken and penned, so He does now, for He is the same now that He was then. So you are to look on the invitations that you find in your Bible not only as invitations that were made then when they were first spoken or written, but that are made now. Christ makes them now as much as He made them then. Those invitations which proceeded out of Christ's mouth when He was on earth are made to you now as much as if they now this moment proceeded from Christ's mouth, for there is no alteration in Christ: He is the same as ever He has been. So when you read or hear any of the invitations of Christ, you may look upon them as if they now came from His blessed lips.

Second, it shows that, if you come to Christ, He will surely prove to be the same in accepting as He is in inviting. Christ will be consistent with Himself. He will not appear one way in calling and inviting you, and then another way in His treatment of you when you come to accept His invitation. Christ will not appear with two faces, with a pleasant winning face in inviting, and with a frowning countenance in His treatment of persons who come at His call; for He is ever the same. You see that Christ is exceedingly gracious and sweet in His invitations; and He surely will be as gracious and sweet in His acceptance of you if you close with His call. And Christ does not merely invite, He also promises that if you accept His invitation He will not reject you. John 6:37: "Him that cometh unto Me I will in no wise cast out." He who is the same yesterday, today, and forever will be found the same in fulfilling what He is in promising.

(2) How Christ has treated those who have come to Him heretofore. Christ in times past has graciously received those who have come to Him. He has made them welcome. He has embraced them in the arms of His love. He has admitted them to a blessed and eternal union with Himself, and has given them a right to all the privileges of the sons of God. And He is the same still that He has been heretofore. We have an account in Scripture of many who came to Him; we have an account in the history of Christ's life of many who accepted His calls, and we have an account in the book of the Acts of the Apostles of multitudes who believed in Him. But we read of none who ever were rejected by Him. And we ourselves have seen many about whom we have reason to think Christ has accepted their coming to Him, many who have been great sinners, many who have been old hardened sinners, many who had been backsliders, and many who had been guilty of quenching the Spirit of God. And He is the

same still: He is as ready to receive such sinners now as He was then. Christ never yet rejected any who came to Him. He has always been the same in this respect. He is so now, and so He surely will be still.

2. There is in this doctrine great encouragement to all persons to look to Christ under all manner of difficulties and afflictions, and that especially from what appeared in Christ when He was here. We have an account in the history of Christ of great numbers, under a great variety of afflictions and difficulties, resorting to Him for help; and we have no account of His rejecting one person who came to Him in a friendly manner for help, under any difficulty whatever. But, on the contrary, the history of His life is principally filled up with miracles that He wrought for the relief of such. When they came to Him, He presently relieved them, and always did it freely without money or price. We never read of His doing anything for any person as hired to it by any reward that was offered Him. And He helped persons fully. He completely delivered them from those difficulties under which they labored. And by the doctrine of the text we learn that though He is not now upon earth, but in heaven, yet He is the same as He was then. He is able to help, and He is as ready to help under every kind of difficulty.

Here is great encouragement for persons who are sick to look to Christ for healing, and for their near friends to carry their case to Christ; for how ready was Christ when on earth to help those who looked to Him under such difficulties! And how sufficient did He appear to be for it, commonly healing by laying on His hand or by speaking a word! And we read of His healing all manner of sickness and all manner of disease among the people. Persons under the most terrible and inveterate diseases were often healed. And Christ is the same still.

And here is great encouragement for mourners to look to Christ for comfort: we read of Christ's pitying such, as in the case of the widow of Nain in Luke 7:12–13. And so He wept with those who wept, and groaned in spirit and wept with compassion for Martha and Mary when He saw their sorrow for the loss of their brother Lazarus (John 11:33). And He is the same still: He is as ready to pity those who are in affliction now as He was then.

And here is great encouragement for those who are exercised with the temptations of Satan; for how often do we read of Christ casting out Satan from those of whom he had the strongest possession! And Christ is the same still. And whoever are under spiritual darkness from the consideration of their own sinfulness have encouragement hence to look to Christ for comfort; for if they do so He will be ready to say to them, as He did to the paralytic in Matthew 9:2, "Son, be of good cheer; thy sins are forgiven thee," for He is still the same as He was then.

USE OF CONSOLATION:

The truth taught in the text may be applied by way of consolation to the godly. You may consider that you have in Him an unchangeable Savior who—as He has loved you and undertaken for you from eternity, and in time has died for you before you were born, and has since converted you by His grace, and brought you out of a blind, guilty, and undone condition, savingly home to Himself—will carry on His work in your heart. He will perfect what is yet lacking in you, in order to your complete deliverance from sin, death, and all evil, and to your establishment in complete and unalterable blessedness. From the unchangeableness of your Savior, you may see how He thinks of that chain in Romans 8:29–30: "For whom He did foreknow, them He also did predestinate; and whom He did predestinate, them He also called; and whom He called, them He also justified; and whom He justified, them He also glorified." The Savior has promised you very great and precious blessings in this world, things which eye has not seen, nor ear heard, nor the heart of man conceived, in the world to come; and from His unchangeableness you may be assured that the things which He has promised He will also perform.

You may from this doctrine see the unchangeableness of His love; and therefore, when you consider how great love He seemed to manifest when He yielded Himself up to God a sacrifice for you in His agony and bloody sweat in the garden, and when He went out to the place of His crucifixion bearing His own cross, you may rejoice that His love now is the same as it was then.

And so when you think of past discoveries which Christ has made of Himself in His glory, and in His love to your soul, you may comfort yourself that He is as glorious, and His love to you is as great, as it was in the time of these discoveries.

You may greatly comfort yourself that you have an unchangeable friend in Christ Jesus. Constancy is justly looked upon as a most necessary and desirable qualification in a friend: that he is not fickle, such that his friendship cannot be depended on as that of a steady, sure friend. How excellent Christ's friendship is you may learn from His manner of treating His disciples on earth, whom He graciously treated as a tender father does his children—meekly instructing them, a most friendly way conversing with them, and being ready to pity them, help them, and forgive their infirmities. And then you may consider this doctrine, and how it thence appears that He is the same still as He was then, and ever will be the same.

From the unchangeableness of your Savior, you may be assured of your continuance in a state of grace. As for yourself, you are so changeable that, if left to yourself, you would soon fall utterly away; there is no depending on your unchangeableness. But Christ is the same, and therefore when He has begun a good work in you He will finish it. As He has been the Author, so He will be the Finisher of your faith. Your love to Christ is in itself changeable, but His to you is unchangeable; and therefore He will never suffer your love to Him utterly to fail. The Apostle gives this reason why the saints' love to Christ cannot fail: that His love to them never can fail.

From the unchangeableness of Christ you may learn the unchangeableness of His intercession, how He will never cease to intercede for you. And from this you may learn the unalterableness of your heavenly happiness. Once you have entered into the happiness of heaven, it never shall be taken from you because Christ, your Savior and Friend, who bestows it on you, and in whom you have it, is unchangeable. He will be the same forever and ever, and therefore so will be your happiness in heaven. As Christ is an unchangeable Savior, so He is your unchangeable portion. This may be your rejoicing, that however your earthly enjoyments may be removed, Christ can never fail. Your dear friends may be taken away and you may suffer many losses, and at last you must part with all those things. Yet you have a portion, a precious treasure, of more worth, ten thousand times more, than all these things. That portion cannot fail you, for you have it in Him who is the same yesterday, today and forever.

The Pure in Heart Blessed

"Blessed are the pure in heart, for they shall see God."
Matthew 5:8

God formerly delivered His law from Mount Sinai by an audible voice, with the sound of a trumpet, with the appearance of devouring fire, with thunder, lightning, and earthquakes. But the principal discoveries of God's Word and will to mankind were reserved to be given by Jesus Christ, His own Son and the Redeemer of men, who is the light of the world.

In this sermon of Christ's, of which the text is a part, we hear Him delivering the mind of God also from a mountain. Here is God speaking as well as from Mount Sinai, and as immediately, but after a very different manner. There God spoke by a preternatural formation of sounds in the air; here He becomes incarnate, takes on Himself our nature, and speaks and converses with us not in a preternatural, awful, and terrible manner, but familiarly as one of us. His face was beheld freely by all who were about Him. His voice was human, without those terrors which made the children of Israel desire that God might speak to them directly no more. And the revelation which He makes of God's Word is more clear and perfect, and more full of the discoveries of spiritual duties, of the spiritual nature of the command of God, of our spiritual and true happiness, and of mercy and grace to mankind. John 1:17: "For the law was given by Moses, but grace and truth came by Jesus Christ."

This discourse of Christ on the Mount seems principally leveled against the false notions and carnal prejudices that were at that day embraced by the nation of Jews; and those benedictions which we have in the beginning of His sermon were sayings that were mere paradoxes to them, wholly contrary to the notions which they had received. That he who was poor in spirit was blessed was a doctrine contrary to the received opinion of the world, and especially of that nation, who were exceedingly ambitious of the praise of men, and highly conceited of their own righteousness. And that he was a blessed and happy man who mourned for sin, and lived mortified to the pleasures and vanities of the world, was contrary to the notions of those who placed their highest happiness in worldly and carnal things. So also, that they who were meek were blessed was another doctrine very contrary to their notions, for they were a very haughty, proud nation, and very vengeful, and maintained the lawfulness of private revenge, as may be seen in the 38th verse. Equally strange to them was the declaration that they who hungered and thirsted after righteousness were happy; for they placed their happiness not in possessing a high degree of righteousness, but in having a great share of worldly goods. They were wont to labor for the meat that perishes; they had no notion of any such thing as spiritual riches, or of happiness in satisfying a spiritual appetite. The Jews were dreadfully in the dark at that day about spiritual things. The happiness which they expected by the Messiah was a temporal and carnal, and not a spiritual, happiness. Christ also tells them that they were blessed who were merciful, and who were peacemakers; which was also a doctrine that the Jews especially stood in need of at that day, for they were generally of a cruel, unmerciful, persecuting spirit.

The truth which Christ teaches them in the text—that they were blessed who were pure in heart—was a thing wholly beyond their conceptions. The Jews at this time placed almost the whole of religion in external things, in a conformity to the rites and ceremonies of the law of Moses. They laid great stress on tithing mint and anise and cumin, and on their traditions, as in washing hands before meat and the like; but they neglected the weightier matters of the law, and especially such as respected holiness of heart. They took much more care to have clean hands and a clean outside than a clean heart, as Christ told them in Matthew 23:25-26: "Woe unto you, scribes and Pharisees, hypocrites! for ye make clean the outside of the cup and of the platter, but within they are full of extortion and excess. Thou blind Pharisee, cleanse first that which is within the cup and platter, that the outside of them may be clean also."

We may observe, concerning the words of the text, that Christ pronounces the pure in heart blessed. Christ here accommodates His instructions to the human nature. He knew that all mankind was in the pursuit of happiness, and He has directed them in the true way to it; and then He tells them what they must become in order to be blessed and happy.

He gives the reason why such are blessed, or wherein the blessedness of such consists: that they shall see God. It is probable that the Jews supposed that it was a great privilege to see God, from those passages in the law where there is an account of Moses' earnestly desiring to see God's glory, and from the account that is given of the seventy elders in Exodus 24:9-11: "Then went up Moses and Aaron, Nadab and Abihu, and seventy of the elders of Israel; and they saw the God of Israel: and there was under His feet as it were a paved work of a sapphire stone, and as it were the body of heaven in His clearness. And upon the nobles of the children of Israel He laid not His hand; also they saw God, and did eat and drink."

It is also probable that they had very imperfect notions of what the vision of God was, and of the happiness that consisted in it, and that their notion of this matter, agreeably to the rest of their carnal, childish notions, was of some outwardly splendid and glorious sight, to please the eye and to entertain the fancy. From these words I shall derive two propositions: it is a truly blessed thing to the soul of man to see God; and to be pure in heart is the certain and only way to attain to this blessedness.

I. It is a truly blessed thing to the soul of man to see God. Here I shall attempt to show:
1. What is meant by seeing God.
First, it is not any sight with the bodily eyes. The blessedness of the soul does not enter in at that door. This would make the blessedness of the soul dependent on the body, or the happiness of man's superior part dependent on the inferior; and this would have confirmed the carnal and childish notions of the Jews.

God is a Spirit, and is not to be seen with the bodily eyes. We find attributed to God that He is invisible. Hebrews 11:27: "As seeing Him who is invisible." Colossians 1:15: "Who is the image of the invisible God." It is mentioned as a part of God's glory in 1 Timothy 1:17: "Now unto the King eternal, immortal, invisible, the only wise God, be honor and glory forever and ever. Amen." That it is not any sight with the bodily eyes is evident because the unembodied souls of the saints see God, and the angels also, who are spirits and were never united to bodies. Matthew 18:10: "Take heed that ye despise not one of these little ones; for I say unto you that in heaven their angels do always behold the face of My Father which is in heaven."

It is not any form or visible representation, nor shape, nor color, nor shining light that is seen, wherein this great happiness of the soul consists. Indeed, God was wont to manifest Himself of old in outward glorious appearances. There was a shining light that was called the glory of the Lord. Thus the glory of the Lord was said to descend on Mount Sinai, and in the tabernacle of the congregation. There was an outward, visible token of God's presence, and the seventy elders, when they saw God in the mount, saw a visible shape. It seems also that when Moses desired to see God's glory, and when God passed by and covered him with His hand in the cleft of the rock, Moses saw some visible glory. Exodus 33:18–20: "And he said, 'I beseech Thee, show me Thy glory.' And He said, 'I will make all My goodness pass before thee, and I will proclaim the name of the Lord before thee; and I will be gracious to whom I will be gracious, and will show mercy on whom I will show mercy.' And He said, 'Thou canst not see My face; for there shall no man see Me and live.'" But it seems that God then condescended to the infant state of the Church, and to the childish notions that were entertained in those days of lesser light. Moses' request seems to have been answered by God making His goodness to pass before him, by proclaiming His name, and by giving him a strong apprehension of the things contained in that name, rather than by showing him any outward glory.

The saints in heaven will behold an outward glory, as they are in the human nature of Christ, which is united to the Godhead, as it is the body of that person who is God; and there will doubtless be appearances of a divine and inimitable glory and beauty in Christ's glorified body, which it will indeed be a refreshing and blessed sight to see.

But the beauty of Christ's body as seen by the bodily eyes will be ravishing and delightful, chiefly as it will express His spiritual glory. The majesty that will appear in Christ's body will express and show forth the spiritual greatness and majesty of the divine nature. The purity and beauty of that light and glory will express the perfection of the divine holiness; the sweetness and ravishing mildness of His countenance will express His divine and spiritual love and grace.

Thus it was when the three disciples beheld Christ at His transfiguration upon the mount. They beheld a wonderful outward glory in Christ's body, an inexpressible beauty in His countenance; but that outward glory and beauty delighted them principally as an expression of divine excellencies of His mind, as we may see from their manner of speaking of it. It was the sweet mixture of majesty and grace in His countenance by which they were ravished. 2 Peter 1:16–18: "We were eyewitnesses of His majesty. For He received from God the Father honor and glory, when there came such a voice to Him from the excellent glory, 'This is My beloved Son, in whom I am well pleased.' And this voice which came from heaven we heard when we were with Him in the holy mount." But especially note the account which John gives of it in John 1:14: "And the Word was made flesh, and dwelt among us, (and we beheld His glory, the glory as of the only-begotten of the Father,) full of grace and truth," where John very probably had in his mind what he had seen in the mount at the transfiguration. Grace and truth are not outward glories, but spiritual ones.

Second, it is an intellectual view by which God is seen. God is a spiritual being, and He is beheld with the understanding. The soul has in itself those powers which are capable of apprehending objects, and especially spiritual objects, without looking through the windows of the outward senses. This is a more perfect way of perception than by the eyes of the body. We are so accustomed and habituated to depend upon our senses, and our intellectual powers are so neglected and disused, that we are ready to conceive that seeing things with the bodily eyes is the most perfect way of apprehending them. But it is not so: the eye of the soul is vastly more perfect than the eye of the body; yet it is not every apprehension of

God by the understanding that may be called the seeing of Him. Some examples are:

(1) There is having an apprehension of God merely by hearsay. If we hear of such a being as God, are educated in the belief that there is such a being, are told what sort of being He is, and what He has done, and are rightly told, and we give credit to what we hear, yet if we have no apprehension of God in any other way we cannot be said to see God in the sense of the text. This is not the beatific sight of God.

(2) We may have an apprehension of God merely by speculative reasoning. If we come to some apprehension of God's being, and of His being almighty, all-wise, and good, by ratiocination, that is not what the Scripture calls seeing God. It is some more immediate way of understanding and viewing that is called sight; nor will such an apprehension as this alone ever make the soul truly blessed.

(3) Nor does every more immediate and sensible apprehension of God qualify as that seeing of Him mentioned in the text and that which is truly beatific. The wicked spirits in the other world have doubtless more immediate apprehensions of the being of God, and of His power and wrath, than the wicked in this world. They stand before God to be judged; they receive the sentence from Him; they have a dreadful apprehension of His wrath and displeasure. But yet they are exceedingly remote from seeing God, in the sense of the text.

But to see God is to have an immediate, sensible, and certain understanding of God's glorious excellency and love.

There must be a direct and immediate sense of God's glory and excellency. I say "direct and immediate" to distinguish it from a mere perception that God is glorious and excellent by means of speculative and distant argumentation, which is a more indirect way of apprehending things. A true sense of the glory of God is that which can never be obtained by speculative ratiocination; and if men convince themselves by argument that God is holy, that never will give a sense of His amiable and glorious holiness. If they argue that He is very merciful, that will not give a sense of His glorious grace and mercy. It must be a more immediate, sensible discovery that gives the mind a real sense of the excellency and beauty of God. He who sees God has a direct and immediate view of God's great and awful majesty, of His pure and beauteous holiness, of His wonderful and endearing grace and mercy. There is a certain understanding of His love; there is a certain apprehension of His presence. He who beholds God does not merely see Him as present by His essence, for so He is present with all, both godly and ungodly. But He is more especially present with those whom He loves. He is graciously present with them, and when they see Him they know Him to be so; they have an understanding of His love to them; they see Him manifesting Himself to them from love. He who has a blessed-making sight of God not only has a view of God's glory and excellency, but he views it as having a property in it. He sees God's love to him; he receives the testimonies and manifestations of that love.

God's favor is sometimes in Scripture called His "face." In Psalm 119:58, where it is translated, "I entreated Thy favor with my whole heart," it is in the original "Thy face." God's hiding His face is a very common expression to signify His withholding the testimonies of His favor.

To see God, as in the text, implies the sight of Him as glorious and gracious; it is a vision of the light of His countenance, both as it is understood of the effulgence of His glory and the manifestations of His favor and love.

The discoveries which the saints have in this world of the glory and love of God are often, in Scripture, called "the sight of God." Thus it is said that Abraham saw Him who is invisible

(Hebrews 11:27). So the saints are said to see as in a glass the glory of the Lord. 2 Corinthians 3:18: "But we all, with open face beholding as in a glass the glory of the Lord, are changed into the same image, from glory to glory, even as by the Spirit of the Lord." Christ speaks of the spiritual knowledge of God. John 14:7: "If ye had known Me, ye would have known My Father also; and from henceforth ye know Him, and have seen Him." The saints in this world have an earnest of what is future; they have the dawnings of future light.

But the more perfect view which the saints have of God's glory and love in another world is what is especially called the seeing of God. Then they shall see Him as He is. That light which now is but glimmering will be brought to clear sunshine; that which is here but the dawning will become perfect day.

Those intellectual views which will be granted in another world are called "seeing God":

First, because the view will be very direct; as when we see things with the bodily eyes. God will, as it were, directly reveal Himself to their minds, so that the understanding shall behold the glory and love of God as a man beholds the countenance of his friend. The discoveries which the saints here have of God's excellency and grace are immediate in a sense: that is, they do not mainly consist in ratiocination. But in another sense they are indirect, that is, they are by means of the gospel as through a glass; but in heaven God will directly excite apprehensions of Himself without the use of any such means.

Second, it is called "seeing" because it will be most certain. When persons see a thing with their own eyes, it gives them the greatest certainty they can have of it, greater than they can have by any information of others. So the sight that they will have in heaven will exclude all doubting. The knowledge of God which the saints have in this world has certainty in it, but yet the certainty is liable to be interrupted with temptations and some degree of doubtings. But there is no such thing in heaven. Looking at the sun does not give a greater or fuller certainty that it shines.

Third, it is called "seeing" because the apprehension of God's glory and love is as clear and lively as when anything is seen with bodily eyes. When we are actually beholding anything with our eyes in the meridian light of the sun, it does not give a more lively idea and apprehension of it than the saints in heaven have of the divine excellency and love of God. When we are looking upon things, our idea is much more clear and perfect, and the impression stronger on the soul, than when we only think of a thing absent. But the intellectual views that the saints in heaven will have of God will go far beyond the advantage of bodily sight; it will be a much more perfect way of apprehending. The saints in heaven will see the glory of the body of Christ after the resurrection with bodily eyes, but they will have no more immediate and perfect way of seeing that visible glory than they will of beholding Christ's divine and spiritual glory. They will not want eyes to see that which is spiritual as well as we can see anything that is corporeal; they will behold God in an ineffable, and to us now inconceivable, manner.

Fourth, the intellectual sight which the saints will have of God will make them as sensible of His presence, and give them as great advantages for conversing with Him, as the sight of the bodily eyes does an earthly friend. Yea, and more too, for when we see our earthly friends with bodily eyes, we have not the most full and direct sight of their principal part, their souls. We see the qualities, dispositions, and acts of their minds in no other way than by outward signs of speech and behavior. Strictly speaking, we do not see the man, the soul, at all, but only its tabernacle or dwelling.

But their souls will have the most clear sight of the spiritual nature of God itself. They shall behold His attributes and disposition towards them more directly, and therefore with greater certainty, than it is possible to see anything in the soul of an earthly friend by his speech and behavior; and therefore their spiritual sight will give them greater advantage for conversing with God than the sight of earthly friends with bodily eyes, or hearing them with our ears, gives us for conversing with them.

2. I shall now give the reasons why thus seeing God is that which will make the soul truly happy.

First, it yields a delight suitable to the nature of an intelligent creature. God has made man, and man only, of all the creatures here below, an intelligent creature; and his reason and understanding are that by which he is distinguished from all inferior ranks of beings. Man's reason is, as it were, a heavenly ray, or, in the language of the wise man, it is "the candle of the Lord" (Proverbs 20:27). It is that wherein mainly consists the natural image of God; it is the noblest faculty of man; it is that which ought to bear rule over the other powers, being given for the end that it might govern the soul.

Therefore, those delights are most suitable to the nature of man that are intellectual, which result from the exercises of this noblest, this distinguishing faculty. God, by giving man understanding, made him capable of such delights, fitted him for them, and designed that such pleasures as those should be his happiness.

Intellectual pleasures consist in beholding spiritual excellencies and beauties, but the glorious excellency and beauty of God are by far the greatest. God's excellence is the supreme excellence. When the understanding of the reasonable creature dwells here, it dwells at the fountain and swims in a boundless, bottomless ocean. The love of God is also the most suitable entertainment of the soul of man, which naturally desires the happiness of society, or of union with some other being. The love of so glorious a being is infinitely valuable, and the discoveries of it are capable of ravishing the soul above all other love. It is suitable to the nature of an intelligent being also, as it is that kind of delight that reason approves of. There are many other delights in which men indulge themselves, which, although they are pleasing to the senses and inferior powers, yet are contrary to reason. Reason opposes the enjoyment of them so that, unless reason is suppressed and stifled, they cannot be enjoyed without a war in the soul. Reason, the noblest faculty, resists the inferior, rebellious powers; and the more reason is in exercise the more will it resist, and the greater will be the inward war and opposition.

But this delight of seeing God the understanding approves of; it is a thing most agreeable to reason that the soul should delight itself in this, and the more reason is in exercise the more it approves of it. So that when it is enjoyed it is with inward peace and a sweet tranquility of soul; there is nothing in human nature that is opposite to it, but everything agrees and conforms to it.

Second, the pleasure which the soul has in seeing God is not only its delight, but it is at the same time its highest perfection and excellency. Man's true happiness is his perfection and true excellency. When any reasonable creature finds that his excellency and his joy are the same thing, then he has come to right and real happiness, and not before. If a man enjoys any kind of pleasure and lives in it, however much he may be taken with what he enjoys, yet, if he is not the more excellent for his pleasures, it is a certain sign that he is not a truly happy man. There are many pleasures that men are wont violently to pursue which are no part of their dignity or perfection, but which, on the contrary, debase the man and make him vile. Instead of rendering the mind beautiful and lovely, they only serve to pollute it; instead of exalting its nature, they make it more akin to that of beasts.

But it is quite the contrary with the pleasure that is to be enjoyed in seeing God. To see God is the highest honor and dignity to which the human nature can attain; that intellectual beholding of Him is itself the highest excellency of the understanding. The great part of the excellency of man is his knowledge and understanding; but the knowledge of God is the most excellent and noble kind of knowledge.

The delight and joy of the soul in that sight are the highest excellency of the other faculty, the will. The heart of man cannot be brought to a higher excellency than to have delight in God, and complacency in the divine excellency and glory. The soul, while it remains under the power of corruption and depravity, cannot have any delight in God's glory. And when its moral relish is so far changed that it is disposed to delight in God's glory, it is most excellently disposed; and when it actually exercises delight in God, it is the most noble and exalted exercise of which it is capable. So that the soul's seeing God, and having pleasure and joy in the sight, is the greatest excellency of both the faculties.

Third, the happiness of seeing God is a blessing without any mixture. That pleasure has the best claim to be called man's true happiness which comes unmixed and without alloy. But so does the joy of seeing God: it neither brings any bitterness, nor will it suffer any.

(1) This pleasure brings no bitterness with it. That is not the case with other delights, in which natural men are wont to place their happiness: they are bitter sweets, yielding a kind of momentary pleasure in gratifying an appetite, but

wormwood and gall are mingled in the cup. He who plucks these roses finds that they grow on thorns; he who tastes of this honey is sure to find in it a sting. If men place their happiness in them, reason and conscience will certainly give them inward disturbance in their enjoyment. There will be the sting of continual disappointments, for carnal delights are of such a nature that they keep the soul that places its happiness in them always big with expectation and in eager pursuit, while they are evermore like shadows, and never yield what is hoped for. They who give themselves up to them unavoidably bring upon themselves many heavy inconveniences. If they promote their pleasure in one way, they destroy their comforts in many other ways; and this sting ever accompanies them: they are but short-lived; they will soon vanish and be no more.

As to the pleasure found in the enjoyment of earthly friends, there is a bitterness that goes also with that. An intense love to any earthly object, though it may afford high enjoyment, yet greatly multiplies our cares and anxieties through the defects and blemishes, the instability and changeableness, of the object; the calamities to which it is exposed; and the short duration of all such friendships, and of the pleasures thence arising.

Some men take a great deal of pleasure in study, in the increase of knowledge; but Solomon, who had great experience, long ago observed that this also is vanity, because he who increases in knowledge increases sorrow. Ecclesiastes 1:17–18: "And I gave my heart to know wisdom, and to know madness and folly: I perceived that this also is vexation of spirit. For in much wisdom is much grief; and he that increaseth knowledge increaseth sorrow." But the delight which the sight of God affords to the soul brings no bitterness with it; there is no disappointment accompanying it; it promises no more than it yields, but, on the contrary, the pleasure is greater than could be imagined before God was seen. It brings no sting of conscience along with it; it brings no vexing care nor anxiety; it leaves no loathing nor distaste behind it.

There is nothing in God which gives uneasiness to him who beholds Him. The view of one attribute adds to the joy that is raised by another. A sight of the holiness of God gives unspeakable pleasure to the mind; the idea of it is a perception beyond measure, the most delightful that can exist in a created mind. And then the beholding of God's grace adds to this joy, for the soul then considers that the Being who is so amiable in Himself is so communicative, so disposed to love and benevolence. The view of the majesty of God greatly heightens this joy—to behold such grace and goodness, and such goodness and majesty united together. Especially will the sight of God's love to Himself, the person beholding, increase the pleasure when he considers that so great and glorious a Being loves him, and is his God and friend. Again, the beholding of God's infinite power will still add to the pleasure, for he reflects that He, who is his friend and loves him with so great a love, can do all things for him. So will the beholding of His wisdom, because He thereby knows what is best for him, and knows how so to order things as shall make him most blessed. So the consideration of His eternity and immutability will make him rejoice to think that his Friend and his Portion is an eternal and unchangeable Friend and Portion. The beholding of God's happiness will increase the joy, to consider that he is so happy who is so much the object of His love. That love of God, in those who shall see God, will cause them exceedingly to rejoice in the happiness of God. Even the sight of God's vindictive justice will add to their joy. This justice of God will appear glorious to them, and will make them prize His love.

(2) This joy is without mixture, not only as it brings not

bitterness with it, but also as it will not suffer any. The sight of God excludes everything that is of a nature different from delight. This light is such as wholly excludes darkness.

It is not in the power of any earthly enjoyment to drive and shut out all trouble from the heart. If a man has some things in which he takes comfort and pleasure, there are others that yield him uneasiness and sorrow. If he has some things in the world that are sweet, there are others that are bitter, against which it is not in the power of his pleasures to help him. We never can find anything here below that shall make us so happy but that we shall have grief and pleasure mixed together. This world, let us make the best of it, will be spotted with black and white, varied with clouds and sunshine, and to them who yield their hearts to it, it will yield pain as well as pleasure. But this pleasure of seeing God can suffer no mixture, for this pleasure of seeing God is so great and strong that it takes the full possession of the heart; it fills it perfectly full, so that there shall be no room for any sorrow, no room in any corner for anything of an adverse nature from joy. There is no darkness that can bear such powerful light. It is impossible that they who see God face to face, who behold His glory and love so immediately as they do in heaven, should have any such thing as grief or pain in their heart. Once the saints have come into God's presence, tears shall be wiped from their eyes, and sorrow and sighing shall flee away. The pleasure will be so great as fully and perfectly to employ every faculty; the sight of God's glory and love will be so wonderful, so engaging to the mind, and it shall keep all the powers of it in such strong attention, that the soul will be wholly possessed and taken up.

(3) Again, there will be in what they shall see a sufficient antidote against everything that would afford uneasiness or that can have any tendency thereto. If there were sin in the

heart before, that used by its exercise to disturb its peace and quiet, and was a seed and spring of trouble, the immediate and full sight of God's glory will at once drive it all away. Sin cannot remain in the heart which thus beholds God, for sin is a principle of enmity against God; but no enmity can remain in one who after this manner sees God's glory. It must and will wholly drive away any such principles, and change it into love. The imperfect sight that the saints have of God's glory here transforms them in part into the same image; but this perfect sight will transform them perfectly. If there is the hatred of enemies, the vision of the love and power of God will be a sufficient antidote against it so that it can give no uneasiness. If the saint is removed by death from all his earthly friends and earthly enjoyments, that will give no uneasiness to him when he sees what a fullness there is in God. He will see that there is all in Him, so that he who possesses Him can lose nothing; whatever is taken from him he sustains no loss. And whatever else there may be, that would otherwise afford grief and uneasiness to the soul, it cannot affect him who is in the presence of God and sees His face.

(4) This joy of seeing God is the true blessedness of man, because the fountain that supplies it is equal to man's desire and capacity.

When God gave man his capacity of happiness, He doubtless made provision for the filling of it. There was some good which God had in His eye when He made the vessel, and made it such dimensions which He knew to be sufficient to fill it; and doubtless that, whatever it is, is man's true blessedness. And that good which is found not to be commensurate to man's capacity and natural desires, and never can equal it, is certainly not that wherein man's happiness consists. Man's desires and capacities are commensurate one with another. Once the capacity is filled, the soul desires no more.

Now in order to judge how great man's capacity is, we must consider the capacity of his principal and leading faculty, his understanding. So great as is the capacity of that faculty, so great is man's capacity of enjoyment; so great a good as the soul is capable of understanding, so great a good it is capable of enjoying. As great a good as the soul is capable of comprehending in its perception and idea, so great a good is it capable of receiving with the other faculty, the will, which keeps pace with the understanding. And that good which the soul can receive with both faculties, of that is it capable of being made the possessor and enjoyer.

But it is easy to perceive that there is nothing here below that can give men such delight as shall be equal to this faculty. Let a man enjoy as great an affluence of earthly comforts as he will, still there is room. Man's nature is capable of a great deal more; there are certain things wanting to which the understanding can extend itself, which he could wish were added.

But the fountain that supplies that joy and delight which the soul has in seeing God is sufficient to fill the vessel because it is infinite. He who sees the glory of God in his measure beholds that of which there is no end. The understanding may extend itself as far as it will; it does but take its flight into an endless expanse and dive into a bottomless ocean. It may discover more and more of the beauty and loveliness of God, but it never will exhaust the fountain. The body of man may as well swallow up the ocean, or his soul embrace immensity, as he can extend his faculties to the utmost of God's excellency.

So in like manner it may be said of the love of God. We can never by soaring and ascending come to the height of it; we can never by descending come to the depth of it, or by measuring know the length and breadth of it. Ephesians

3:18–19: "That ye may be able to comprehend with all saints what is the breadth, and length, and depth, and height; and to know the love of Christ, which passeth knowledge, that ye might be filled with all the fullness of God." So that, let the thoughts and desires extend themselves as they will, here is space enough for them in which they may expand forever. How blessed therefore are they who see God, who have come to this inexhaustible fountain! They have obtained that delight which gives full satisfaction. Having come to this pleasure, they neither do nor can desire any more. They can sit down fully contented, and take up with this enjoyment forever and ever and desire no change. After they have had the pleasure of beholding the face of God for millions of ages, it will not grow into a dull story. The relish of this delight will be as exquisite as ever; there is enough still for the utmost employment of every faculty.

(5) This delight in the vision of God has an unfailing foundation. God made man to endure forever, and therefore that which is man's true blessedness we may conclude has a sure and lasting foundation. As for worldly enjoyments, their foundation is a sandy one that is continually wearing away, and certainly will at last let the building fall. If we take pleasure in riches, riches in a little while will be gone; if we take pleasure in gratifying our senses, those objects whence we draw our gratifications will perish with the using, and our senses themselves also will be gone, the organs will be worn out, and our whole outward form will turn to dust. If we take pleasure in union with our earthly friends, that union must be broken; the bonds are not durable, but will soon wear asunder.

But he who has the immediate intellectual vision of God's glory and love, and rejoices in that, has his happiness built upon an everlasting rock. Isaiah 26:4: "Trust ye in the Lord forever, for in the Lord Jehovah is everlasting strength." In the Hebrew it is, "in the Lord Jehovah is the Rock of ages."

The glory of God is subject to no changes nor vicissitudes; it will never cease to shine forth. History gives us an account of the sun's light failing, and becoming more faint and dim for many months together; but the glory of God will never be subject to fading. Of the light of that Sun there never will be any eclipse or dimness, but it will shine eternally in its strength. Isaiah 60:19: "The sun shall be no more thy light by day, neither for brightness shall the moon give light unto thee; but the Lord shall be unto thee an everlasting light, and thy God thy glory." So the love of God toward those who see His face will never fail or be subject to any abatement. He loves His saints with an everlasting love. Jeremiah 31:3. "The Lord hath appeared of old unto me, saying, 'Yea, I have loved thee with an everlasting love; therefore with loving-kindness have I drawn thee.' " Those streams of pleasure which are at God's right hand are never dry, but ever flowing and ever full.

How much does the sense of the sureness of this foundation confirm and heighten the joy! The soul enjoys its delight in a sense of this, free from all fears and jealousies, and with an unspeakable quietness and assurance. Isaiah 32:17: "And the work of righteousness shall be peace; and the effect of righteousness, quietness and assurance forever."

From this part of the subject we may derive several important and useful reflections.

1. Here we may see one instance wherein the revelation of Jesus Christ excels all human wisdom. It was a thing that had been beyond the wisdom of the world to tell wherein man's true happiness consisted; there was a vast variety of opinions about it among the wise men and philosophers of the heathen. Indeed, on no other subject was there so great difference among them. If I remember right, there were several

hundred different opinions reckoned up respecting it, which shows that they were woefully in the dark. Though there were many very wise men among them, men famed through all succeeding ages for their knowledge and wisdom, yet their reason was not sufficient to find out man's true happiness.

We can give reasons for it now that it is revealed, and it seems so rational that one would think the light of nature sufficient to discover it; but we, having always lived in the enjoyment of gospel light and being accustomed to it, are hardly sensible how dependent we are upon it, and how much we should be in the dark about things that now seem plain to us, if we never had had our reason assisted by revelation.

God has made foolish the wisdom of this world by the gospel. 1 Corinthians 1:20: "Where is the wise? Where is the scribe? Where is the disputer of this world? Hath not God made foolish the wisdom of this world?" That is, He has shown the foolishness of their wisdom by this brighter light of His revelation. For all that philosophy and human wisdom could do, it was the gospel that first taught the world wherein mankind's true blessedness consisted, and that taught them the way to attain to it.

2. Hence we learn the great privilege we have who possess such advantages to come to the blessedness of seeing God. We have the true God revealed to us in the Word of God, who is the Being in the sight of whom this happiness is to be enjoyed. We have the glorious attributes and perfections of God declared to us. The glory of God in the face of Jesus Christ is discovered in the gospel which we enjoy. His beauties and glories are there, as it were, pointed forth by God's own hand to our view; so that we have those means which God has provided for our obtaining those beginnings of this sight of Him which the saints have in this world in that spiritual knowledge which they have of God, which is absolutely necessary in order

for us to have it perfectly in another world.

The knowledge which believers have of God and His glory, as appearing in the face of Christ, is the imperfect beginning of this heavenly sight. It is an earnest of it; it is the dawning of the heavenly light; and this beginning must evermore precede or a perfect vision of God in heaven cannot be obtained. And all those who have this beginning shall obtain that perfection also. Great therefore is our privilege that we have the means of this spiritual knowledge. We may in this world see God as in a glass darkly, in order to our seeing Him hereafter face to face; and surely our privilege is very great that He has given us that glass from whence God's glory is reflected. We have not only the discoveries of God's glory in the doctrines of His Word, but we have abundant directions how to act so that we may obtain a perfect and beatific sight of God, one of which we have in our text, and of which I shall speak particularly hereafter.

3. This doctrine may lead us to a sense of the blessedness of the heavenly state, and justly cause us to long after it. In heaven the saints see God; they enjoy that vision of Him of which we have been speaking in its perfection. All clouds and darkness are there removed; they there behold the glory and love of God more immediately, and with greater certainty and a more strong and lively apprehension than a man beholds his friend when he is with him, and sees his face by the noonday sun, and with far greater advantages for conversation and enjoyment.

Well may this make the heavenly state appear a blessed state to us, and make us breathe after it. Well may the consideration of these things make the saints wait for and desire their happy change. Well may it make them long for the appearing of Christ. This they know, that when He shall appear they shall see Him as He is. 1 John 3:2: "Beloved, now are we the sons of God, and it doth not yet appear what we shall be; but we know that when He shall appear, we shall be like Him, for we shall see Him as He is."

This may well be comforting to the saints under the apprehensions of death, and it is a consideration sufficient to take away the sting of it and uphold them while walking through the midst of that valley. This also may well comfort and uphold them in all troubles and difficulties they meet with here, that after a little while they shall see God; which will immediately dry up all tears, drive away all sorrow and sighing, and expel forever every darksome thought from the heart.

4. Hence we learn that a life of holiness is the pleasantest life in this world, because in such a life we have the imperfect beginnings of a blessed and endless sight of God. And so they have something of true happiness while here, they have the seeds of blessedness sown in their souls, and they begin to shoot forth.

As for all others, those who do not live a holy life have nothing at all of true happiness because they have nothing of the knowledge of God.

II. To be pure in heart is the certain and only way to attain to this blessedness.

We have shown what this seeing of God is, and have represented in some measure how great is the blessedness of so seeing Him. And if what we have heard is believed and cordially received by us, it will be sufficient to awaken our attention to any instructions from the Word of God that are to point out the way to us wherein we may attain to this blessedness.

If men should hear of some vast estate, or some rich hidden treasure, and at the same time should hear of some very feasible way in which they might make it all their own, how ready would they be to hear; with what eagerness would they listen to those who should bring such news and give them such directions, provided they had reason to believe that what was told them was true! We are here told of a much truer and greater blessedness than any treasure of silver, and gold, and pearls can yield; and we are also told of the way whereby we may assuredly become the possessors of it by Him who certainly knows. I shall show (1) what it is to be pure in heart; (2) that to be pure in heart is the sure way to gain this blessedness; (3) that it is the only way.

1. I shall inquire what it is to be pure in heart. Purity of heart is here to be understood in distinction from a mere external purity, or a purity of the outward actions and behavior in those things that appear to men in an external morality, an outward attendance on ordinances, a profession of the true religion and pure doctrines, and a making an outward show and appearance of godliness.

Christ very probably had in our text an eye to the formality and hypocrisy of the scribes and Pharisees, and other great saints, as they accounted themselves, and were accounted among the Jews. These were exceedingly exact in their observance of the ordinances of the ceremonial law; they were careful not to deviate from it in the least punctilio. For instance, how exact were they in observing the law of tithes; they were careful to bring the tenth of the herbs in their gardens—mint, anise, and cumin. They were very careful to keep themselves from all ceremonial uncleanness, and they even added to the law in this particular: they were for being stricter and purer than the law required, and therefore made it a point of conscience to wash their hands before every meal. They were very strict to avoid conversing with the Samaritans; they would not eat with them, nor have any dealings with them, lest they should be defiled. They used to say to other nations, "Stand by thyself, come not nigh, for I am holier than thou." They looked upon themselves only as pure, because they were the children of Abraham, and because they were circumcised and attended to the ceremonial law; because they made clean the outside of the cup and the platter, and because of their external purity, they looked upon themselves as the peculiar favorites of heaven, and expected to be admitted to see God, when all the uncircumcised, and those who were not the children of Abraham, would be excluded.

But Christ corrected their mistake, and taught that such an external purity will never give a man a title to this blessedness, for it is purity of heart that is requisite in order to attain to it. Matthew 5:20: "For I say unto you that except your righteousness shall exceed the righteousness of the scribes and Pharisees, ye shall in no case enter into the kingdom of heaven."

However exact any man may be in the external observance of moral, instituted duties, if he is careful to wrong no man, and can say, as the young Pharisee did, "All these have I kept from my youth," i.e., as to an external observance; if he is very strict in keeping the sabbath and in coming to the house of God, in attending to family and secret prayer, yet if he has not holiness of heart he is never likely to see God. It is no reformation of manners that is sufficient, but there must be a new heart and a right spirit. It is the heart that God requires. Proverbs 23:26: "My son, give Me thine heart." It is the heart that God looks at. However fair and pure an outside there may be that may be very pleasing to men, yet if there is not purity of heart the man is not at all the more acceptable to God. 1 Samuel 16:7: "But the Lord said unto Samuel, 'Look not on his countenance, or on the height of his stature, because I have refused him; for the Lord seeth not as man seeth; for man looketh on the outward appearance, but the Lord looketh on the heart.' " If men outwardly behave well and speak well, yet it is not accepted without trying and weighing the heart. Proverbs 16:2: "All the ways of a man are clean in his own eyes, but the Lord weigheth the spirits." It is the spirit which is the subject of this blessedness of seeing God, and therefore the qualities of the spirit, and not so much those of the outward man, are regarded.

Now the heart is said to be pure in the sense of the text:

First, with respect to the spiritual defilement from which it is pure;

Second, with respect to certain positive qualities that it is endowed with.

The word "pure," in its common acceptance, merely signifies something negative, the absence of all mixture or defilement; but in pureness of heart, as it is used in Scripture, seems to be implied both something negative and positive—not only the absence or removal of defilement, but also positive qualities that are called "pure."

First, the heart is said to be pure with respect to the filthiness from which it is pure. Sin is the greatest filthiness. There is nothing that can so defile and render so abominable. It is that which has an infinite abominableness in it; and indeed it is the only spiritual defilement. There is nothing else that can defile the soul. Now there are none in this life who are pure from sin in such a sense that there is no remainder, no mixture of sin. Proverbs 20:9: "Who can say, 'I have made my heart clean, I am pure from my sin'?" So that if this were the requisite qualification, none of the children of men would ever come to see God.

But the purity of heart, with respect to sin, that may be obtained in this life consists in the following things:

(1) It implies that the soul sees the filthiness that there is in sin, and accordingly abhors it. Sin, which is so filthy in it-

self, is become so sensibly to the man whose heart is pure; he sees its odiousness and deformity, and it is become nauseous to him.

To those animals which are of a filthy and impure nature, as swine and dogs, ravens and vermin, those things that are filthy and nauseous to mankind do not seem at all disgusting, but on the contrary they love them; it is food that suits their appetites. It is because they are of an impure and filthy nature. The nature of the animal is agreeable to such things.

So it is with men of impure hearts. They see no filthiness in sin; they are not nauseated by it; it is in no way uncomfortable to them to have it hanging about them; they can wallow in it without any reluctance. Yea, they take pleasure in it. It is their meat and their drink, because they are of an impure nature. But he who has become pure in heart hates sin. He has an antipathy to it. He does not love to be near it. If he sees any of it hanging about him, he abhors himself for it. He seems filthy to himself; he is a burden to himself; he abhors the very sight of it, and shuns the appearance of it. If he sees sin in others, it is a very unpleasant sight to him. As sin, and as it is committed against God, it is grievous and uncomfortable to him wherever he discovers it. It is because his heart is changed, and God has given him a pure nature.

(2) It implies godly sorrow for sin. The pure heart has not only respect to that spiritual filthiness that is present, to abhor it and shun it, but it has also respect to past sin. The consideration of that grieves it; it causes shame and sorrow to think that it ever rejoiced in such defilement, that it ever was so abominable as to love and feed upon it. Every transgression leaves a filth behind it on the soul, and this remaining filth occasions pain to the renewed and purified heart. By godly sorrow the heart exerts itself against the filthiness of past sins, and endeavors to cast it off and purge itself from it.

(3) It implies that sin is mortified in the heart, so that it is free from the reigning power and dominion of it. Though the heart is not perfectly free from all sin, yet a freedom is begun. Before, spiritual filth had the possession of the heart, corruption had the entire government of the soul, and every faculty was so wholly defiled by it that all its acts were filthy, and only filthy—the heart was entirely enslaved to sin.

But now the power of sin is broken and the strong bands by which it was tied and fastened to the heart are in a great measure loosed, so that corruption has no longer the possession and government of the heart as before. The principal seat, the throne of the heart, that was formerly possessed by corruption is now purged, and filthiness does now, as it were, only possess the interior and exterior parts of the soul. John 13:10: "He that is washed needeth not, save to wash his feet."

(4) The heart that is pure will be continually endeavoring to cleanse itself from all remaining filthiness. Though there are remains of impurity, yet the new nature is so contrary to it that it will never rest or be quiet, but will always be cleansing itself. Like a vessel of fermenting liquor, it will continue working till it has worked itself clear, and cast off all the filth and sediment. Or like a stream of good water, if the water is in itself sweet and good, however it may be defiled from the muddy banks, it will refine as it runs, and will run itself clear again; but the fountain that yields impure water will never cleanse itself. So he who is pure in heart will never suffer himself to live in any sin. If he is overtaken in a fault, he will return and cleanse himself again by repentance and reformation, and a more earnest care that he may avoid that sin for the future.

The remaining corruption that is in his heart will be his great and continual burden, and he will be endeavoring to cleanse himself more and more. He will not rest in any supposed degree of purity so long as he sees any degree of impurity remaining, but he will be striving after progress in the mortification of sin and in the increase of holiness.

(5) The heart is said to be pure, especially with respect to its cleanness from, and opposition to, the lust of uncleanness. This kind of wickedness we find to be more especially called uncleanness and filthiness in Scripture; it brings a peculiar turpitude upon the soul and defiles the temple of God. 1 Corinthians 3:17: "If any man defile the temple of God, him shall God destroy; for the temple of God is holy, which temple ye are." Pureness in Scripture is sometimes used only in this restrained sense, with respect to freedom from fleshly impurities. So it seems to be in Philippians 4:8: "Finally, brethren, whatsoever things are true, whatsoever things are honest, whatsoever things are just, whatsoever things are pure, whatsoever things are lovely, whatsoever things are of good report; if there be any virtue, and if there be any praise, think on these things."

Now this sort of purity of heart is absolutely necessary in order to our coming to see God. There must be a renunciation of all impure and lascivious practices and conversation. They who live in the indulgence of such a lust in one kind of practice or another, or though it is only with their eyes or in their thoughts, are of impure hearts, and shall never come to see God unless they have new hearts given them.

They who have pure hearts abhor and are afraid of such things (Jude 23). They take heed that they do not prostitute their souls to so much as mental and imaginary sins, much less to practical impurities and works of darkness.

Second, the heart is said to be pure in respect to its being endowed with positive qualities that are of a contrary nature to spiritual filthiness.

Though purity in strictness is only a freedom from filth,

yet there are positive qualities of mind that seem to be implied in purity of heart, which may be reckoned a part of it because of their contrariety to filthiness. The heart, by reason of them, is still more remote from defilement, as a greater light may be said to be purer than a lesser; for although the lesser light has no mixture of darkness, yet the greater light is still more remote from darkness.

He is pure in heart who delights in holy exercises. Those exercises that are holy are natural and pleasant to him; he sees the beauty there is in holiness, and that beauty has such a strong influence upon his heart that he is captivated thereby. He delights in the pure and holy exercise of love to God, in the fear of God, in praising and glorifying God, and in pure and holy love to men. He delights in holy thoughts and meditations. Those exercises of the understanding that are holy are most agreeable to him, as are those exercises of the will. Such inclinations, desires, and affections are most delightful which are spiritual and holy.

He is pure in heart who chooses and takes the greatest delight in spiritual enjoyment. A spiritual appetite is that which governs in his soul, and carries him above the mean lust and defiled enjoyments of this world towards spiritual and heavenly objects. The enjoyment which he chooses and chiefly desires, such as seeing God and enjoying communion with Him, are enjoyments of the most refined and pure nature. He hungers and thirsts after the pure light of the new Jerusalem.

2. To be pure in heart is the sure way to obtain the blessedness of seeing God. This is the divine road to the blissful and glorious presence of God, which, if we take it, will infallibly lead us there.

God is the giver of the pure heart, and He gives it for this very end: that it may be prepared for the blessedness of seeing

Him. Thus we are taught in the Scriptures. The people of God are sanctified, and their hearts are made pure, that they may be prepared for glory as vessels are prepared by the potter for the use he designs. They are elected from all eternity to eternal life, and have purity of heart given them on purpose to fit them for that to which they are chosen. Romans 9:23: "And that He might make known the riches of His glory on the vessels of mercy, which He had afore prepared to glory."

We read of the Church being arrayed in fine linen, clean and white, by which is signified the Church's purity; and it was to fit it for the enjoyment of Christ. Revelation 19:7–8: "Let us be glad and rejoice, and give honor to Him; for the marriage of the Lamb is come, and His wife hath made herself ready. And to her was granted that she should be arrayed in fine linen, clean and white; for the fine linen is the righteousness of the saints." And in Revelation 21:2, the Church thus purified is said to be as a bride adorned for her husband: "And I, John, saw the holy city, new Jerusalem, coming down from God out of heaven, prepared as a bride adorned for her husband." Therefore if God gives the pure heart to fit and prepare us for the vision of Himself, He will obtain His own end; for who can prevent Him from doing what He purposes?

God also has promised it. He has given His faithful word for it in our text. To the same purpose is Psalm 24:3–4: "Who shall ascend into the hill of the Lord? Or who shall stand in His holy place? He that hath clean hands, and a pure heart; who hath not lifted up his soul unto vanity, nor sworn deceitfully." And Isaiah 33:15–17: "He that walketh righteously, and speaketh uprightly: he that despiseth the gain of oppression, that shaketh his hands from holding of bribes, that stoppeth his ears from hearing of blood, and shutteth his eyes from seeing evil—he shall dwell on high: his place of defense shall be the munition of rocks; bread shall be given him; his water shall be sure. Thine eyes shall see the King in His beauty; they shall behold the land that is very far off."

3. This is the only way to come to this blessedness.

First, it is in no way fit or suitable that those who have not pure hearts, should be admitted to this privilege. It should be most unsuitable for those who are defiled all over with the most loathsome filth to be admitted into the glorious presence of the King of heaven and earth. It would not become the majesty of God to allow those who are so abominable to come into His blessed presence; nor is it at all becoming His holiness, whereby He is of purer eyes than to behold such pollution.

It becomes persons, when they come into the presence of a king, so to attire themselves that they may not appear in a sordid habit; and it would be much more unsuitable still for any to come all defiled with filth. But sin is that which renders the soul much more loathsome in the sight of God. This spiritual filth is of a nature most disagreeable to that pure, heavenly light; it would be most unsuitable to have the pollution of sin and wickedness and the light of glory mixed together; and it is what God never will suffer. It would be a most unbecoming thing for such to be the objects of God's favor, and to see the love of God, and to receive the testimonies of that love. It would be most unsuitable for the glorious and most blessed God to embrace in the arms of His love that which is infinitely more filthy than a reptile.

Second, it is naturally impossible that the soul which is impure should see God. The sight of God's glory and impurity of heart are not compatible in the same subject. Where spiritual defilement holds possession of the heart, it is impossible that the divine light which reveals God's glory should enter. How can he who is under the power of enmity against

God, and who only hates God, see His beauty and loveliness at the same time? Sin, so long as it has the government and possession of the soul, will blind the mind and maintain darkness. As long as sin keeps possession, the heart will be blinded through its deceitfulness.

Third, if it were possible for them to see God, they could not find any blessedness in it. What pleasure would it give to the soul that hates holiness to see the holiness of God; what pleasure would it give to those who are God's enemies to see His greatness and glory? Wicked men have no relish for such intellectual, pure, and holy delights and enjoyments. As we have observed already, to have a relish for spiritual enjoyments is one part of the purity of heart spoken of in the text.

Fourth, it is impossible that such should be the objects of God's favor and complacence, and therefore they cannot have this part of the blessed-making vision of God: the seeing of His love. It is impossible that God should take pleasure in wickedness or have complacence in the wicked; and therefore they cannot have the blessed-making vision of God, for seeing the love of God is an essential part of it. If a man sees how glorious God is, and has not this consideration with it, that he has a property in this glory of God; if he cannot consider this glorious being as his Friend; if he takes no pleasure in Him, but, on the contrary, loathes and abhors Him, the sight of God will be to him no blessedness.

Application

1. Hence we learn how great a thing it is to be an upright and sincere Christian; for all such are pure in heart, and stand entitled to the blessedness of seeing the most high God. The time is coming when they shall assuredly see Him; they shall see Him who is infinitely greater than all the kings of the

earth; they shall see Him face to face, shall see as much of His glory and beauty as the eyes of their souls are capable of beholding. They shall not only see Him for a few moments or an hour, but they shall dwell in His presence, and shall sit down forever to drink in the rays of His glory. They shall see Him invested in all His majesty, with smiles and love in His countenance. They shall see Him and converse with Him as their nearest and best Friend.

Thus shall they see Him soon. The intervening moments fly swiftly; the time is even at the door, when they shall be admitted to this blessedness.

2. Let the consideration of this subject put us all upon inquiring whether we ourselves are pure in heart. Is our religion of that kind which has its seat chiefly in the heart, or does it chiefly consist in what is outward in morality and formality? Have we ever experienced a change of heart? Have we a right spirit renewed within us? Have we ever seen the odiousness and filthiness that there is in sin? Is it what we hate, wherever we see it; and do we especially hate it in ourselves, and loathe ourselves for it? Is it the object of our hatred as sin, and as it is against God?

Are there any who now hear me who think themselves to be Christians, who do yet, either in their imaginations and thoughts or in any secret practice, allow and indulge the lust of uncleanness and live in such a way? If it is so, they have great need to think with themselves whether or not they are of that generation who are pure in their own eyes, and yet are not cleansed from their filthiness. If they imagine that they are pure in heart and live in such wickedness, their confidence is vain presumption. Inquire whether holy exercises and holy employments are the delight of your soul, and what you take pleasure in above all other things in which you can be engaged. Are the enjoyments that you choose and take the greatest delight in spiritual and heavenly enjoyments? Is seeing God, conversing with Him, and dwelling in His presence forever what you would, of your own accord, choose above all other things?

3. I would earnestly exhort those who hear me to make for themselves a pure heart. Though it is God's work to give it, yet it is as truly your work to obtain it; though it is God's work to purify the heart, yet the actual, or rather the active, procuring of it is your act. All pure and holy exercises are man's acts, and they are his duty. Therefore we are commanded to make us a new heart, and a right spirit. Ezekiel 18:31: "Cast away from you all your transgressions, whereby ye have transgressed, and make you a new heart and a new spirit; for why will ye die?"

We must not think to excuse ourselves by saying that it is God's work, and that we cannot purify our own hearts; for though it is God's work in one sense, yet it is equally our work in another. James 4:8: "Draw nigh to God, and He will draw nigh to you. Cleanse your hands, ye sinners, and purify your hearts, ye double-minded." If you do not engage in this work yourselves and purify your own hearts, they never will be pure. If you do not get a pure heart, the blame of it will be laid to your own backwardness. The unclean soul hates to be purified; it is opposite to its nature; there is a great deal of self-denial in it. But be content to contradict the nature and bent of your own heart that it may be purified; however grating it may be to you at first, yet consider how blessed the issue will be. Though the road is a little rough in the beginning, yet it will grow more and more pleasant, till at last it will infallibly lead to that lightsome and glorious country, the inhabitants of which see and converse with God. Proverbs 4:18: "But the path of the just is as the shining light that shineth more and more unto the perfect day." If you would be on the way to having a pure heart:

1. Purify your hands. Cleanse yourself from every external impurity of speech and behavior; take heed that you never defile your hands in known wickedness; break off all your sins by righteousness; and take heed that you do not give way to impure lusts that would entice to sinful actions. If you set about the work of cleansing yourself, but when a temptation comes you plunge yourself into the mire again, you never will be likely to become pure; but you must be steady in your reformation, and in the amendment of your ways and doings.

2. Take heed that you do not rest in external purity, but seek purity of heart in the ways of God's appointment. Seek it in a constant and diligent attendance on all God's ordinances.

3. Be often searching your own heart, and seek and pray that you may see the filthiness of it. If ever you are made pure, you must be brought to see that you are filthy; you must see the plague and pollution of your own heart.

4. Beg of God that He would give you His Holy Spirit. It is the Spirit of God that purifies the soul. Therefore the Spirit of God is often compared to fire, and is said to baptize with fire. He cleanses the heart as fire cleanses the metals, and burns up the filth and pollution of the mind, and is therefore called the "spirit of burning." Isaiah 4:4: "When the Lord shall have washed away the filth of the daughters of Zion, and shall have purged the blood of Jerusalem from the midst thereof by the spirit of judgment, and by the spirit of burning."

Christ the Example of Ministers

"For I have given you an example that ye should do as I have done to you. Verily, verily I say unto you, the servant is not greater than his lord, neither he that is sent greater than he that sent him." John 13:15–16

We have in the context an account of one of the many very remarkable things that passed that night wherein Christ was betrayed (which was on many accounts the most remarkable night that ever was), Christ's washing His disciples' feet. This action, as it was exceedingly wonderful itself, so it manifestly was symbolic, and represented something else far more important and more wonderful—even that greatest and most wonderful of all things that ever came to pass, which was accomplished the next day in His last sufferings. There were three symbolic representations given of that great event this evening: one in the Passover, which Christ now partook of with His disciples; another in the Lord's Supper, which He instituted at this time; and another in this remarkable action of His washing His disciples' feet. Washing the feet of guests was the office of servants, and one of their meanest offices; therefore it was fitly chosen by our Savior to represent that great abasement which He was to be the subject of in the form of a servant, in becoming obedient unto death, even that ignominious and accursed death of the cross, that He might cleanse the souls of His disciples from their guilt and spiritual pollution.

This spiritual washing and cleansing of believers was the

end for which Christ so abased Himself for them. Titus 2:14: "Who gave Himself for us, that He might redeem us from all iniquity, and purify unto Himself a peculiar people." Ephesians 5:25–26: "Christ loved the church, and gave Himself for it, that He might sanctify and cleanse it with the washing of water." That Christ's washing His disciples' feet signified this spiritual washing of the soul is manifest by His own words in John 13:8: "Peter saith unto Him, 'Thou shalt never wash my feet.' Jesus answered him, 'If I wash thee not, thou hast no part with Me.' " Christ, in being obedient unto death, even the death of the cross, not only did the part of a servant unto God, but in some respects also of a servant unto us. And this is not the only place where His so abasing Himself for our sakes is compared to the doing of the part of a servant to guests. We have the like representation made in Luke 22:27: "For which is greater, he that sitteth at meat, or he that serveth? Is not he that sitteth at meat? But I am among you as He that serveth." And wherein Christ was among the disciples as He who served is explained in Matthew 20:28, namely, in His giving His life as a ransom for them.

When Christ had finished washing His disciples' feet, He solemnly required their attention to what He had done, and commanded them to follow His example therein. John 13:12–17: "So after He had washed their feet, and had taken His garments, and was set down again, He said unto them, 'Know ye what I have done unto you? Ye call Me Master and Lord, and ye say well, for so I am. If I then, your Lord and Master, have washed your feet, ye also ought to wash one another's feet; for I have given you an example, that ye should do as I have done to you. Verily, verily, I say unto you, the servant is not greater than his lord, neither he that is sent greater than he that sent him. If ye know these things, happy are ye if ye do them.' "

When our Savior called on His disciples to imitate the example He had given them in what He had done, we are to understand not merely by the example He gave in the emblematic action in washing His disciples' feet in itself considered, but more especially of that much greater act of His that was signified by it in abasing Himself so low, and suffering so much, for the spiritual cleansing and salvation of His people.

This is what is chiefly insisted on as the great example Christ has given us to follow. So it is once and again afterwards in the discourse Christ had with His disciples, this same night, in verse 34 of the same chapter: "A new commandment I give unto you, that ye love one another; as I have loved you, that ye also love one another." John 15:12–13: "This is My commandment, that ye love one another, as I have loved you. Greater love hath no man than this, that a man lay down his life for his friends." And so 1 John 3:16: "Hereby perceive we the love of God, because He laid down His life for us; and we ought to lay down our lives for the brethren."

Christ, in the words of the text, not only intends to recommend this example of His to the disciples as Christians, or some of His professing people, but especially as His ministers. This is evident by those words He used to enforce this counsel: "Neither he that is sent is greater than he that sent him." In these words He manifestly has respect to that great errand on which He had sent them, when He bid them go and preach the gospel to the lost sheep of the house of Israel (Matthew 10:5–6), and on which they were to be sent after His resurrection when He said to them, "Go ye into all the world, and preach the gospel to every creature" (Mark 16:15). This same errand Christ has respect to in John 20:21: "As My Father hath sent Me, even so send I you."

And what confirms this is that Christ elsewhere recommends to officers in His Church, who are in that respect chief among His followers, the example which He set in His abasing Himself to be as a servant who ministers to guests at a table, in His giving His life for us. Matthew 20:27–28: "Whosoever will be chief among you, let him be your servant—even as the Son of Man came not to be ministered unto, but to minister, and to give His life a ransom for many." Compare this with Luke 22:25–28.

The work and business of ministers of the gospel is, as it were, that of servants: to wash and cleanse the souls of men; for this is done by the preaching of the Word, which is their main business. Ephesians 5:26: "That He might sanctify and cleanse it with the washing of water by the Word." The words of the text thus considered undoubtedly lead us to this conclusion, and teach us:

DOCTRINE: It is the duty of ministers of the gospel, in the work of their ministry, to follow the example of their great Lord and Master.

This is what I would by divine assistance make the subject of my present discourse. And I propose to handle this subject in the following method. I would:

I. Observe wherein ministers of the gospel ought to follow the example of Christ;

II. Give some reasons why they should follow His example;

III. Endeavor to make a proper application of those things to myself, and others who are called to this work of the ministry; and

IV. Show what improvement should be made of them by the people of this church and congregation.

I. I would show wherein ministers of the gospel ought, in the work of their ministry, to follow the example of their great Lord and Master, Jesus Christ.

1. In general, ministers should follow their Lord and

Master in all those excellent virtues, and in that universal and eminent holiness of life, which He set an example of in this human nature.

The ministers of Christ should be persons of the same spirit that their Lord was, the same spirit of humility and lowliness of heart; for the servant is not greater than his Lord. They should be of the same spirit of heavenly-mindedness, and contempt of the glory, wealth, and pleasures of this world; they should be of the same spirit of devotion and fervent love to God; they should follow the example of His prayerfulness. We read from time to time of His retiring from the world, away from the noise and applause of the multitudes, into mountains and solitary places for secret prayer and holy converse with His Father. We read once of His rising up in the morning a great while before day, and going and departing into a solitary place to pray (Mark 1:35). And we read another time of His going out into a mountain to pray, and continuing all night in prayer (Luke 6:12).

Ministers should follow Christ's example in His strict, constant, and inflexible observance of the commands which God had given Him touching what He should do and what He should say. He spoke nothing of Himself, but those things which the Father had commanded Him, those He spoke, and always did those things that pleased Him. He continued in thorough obedience in the greatest trials, and through the greatest opposition that ever there was any instance of. Ministers should be persons of the same quiet, lamb-like spirit that Christ was of, the same spirit of submission to God's will, and patience under afflictions, and meekness towards men; of the same calmness and composure of spirit under reproaches and sufferings from the malignity of evil men; of the same spirit of forgiveness of injuries; of the same spirit of charity, of fervent love and extensive benevolence; the same disposition to pity the miserable, to weep with those who weep, to help men under their calamities of both soul and body, to hear and grant the requests of the needy, and relieve the afflicted; the same spirit of condescension to the poor and mean, tenderness and gentleness towards the weak, and great and effectual love to enemies. They should also be of the same spirit of zeal, diligence, and self-denial for the glory of God, and advancement of His kingdom, and for the good of mankind; for which things' sake Christ went through the greatest labors and endured the most extreme sufferings.

2. More particularly should ministers of the gospel follow the example of their great Master in the manner in which they seek the salvation and happiness of the souls of men. They should follow His example of love to souls. Though it be impossible that they should love them to so great a degree, yet they should have the same spirit of love to them, and concern for their salvation, according to their capacity. Love to men's souls in Christ was far above any regard He had to His temporal interest, His ease, His honor, His meat and drink; and so it should be with His ministers. They should have the same spirit of compassion to men under their spiritual calamities and miseries that He had, of whom we read in Mark 6:34: "When He came out and saw much people, He was moved with compassion towards them, because they were as sheep not having a shepherd; and He began to teach them many things." The word translated "moved with compassion" signifies that He was most sensibly affected, and His inmost bowels moved with pity. And again we read in Luke 19 that when Christ was riding to Jerusalem, that wicked city, but a few days before His crucifixion, and was come to the descent of the Mount of Olives, where He had a fair view of the city, when He beheld it, He wept over it on account of the misery and ruin they had brought themselves into danger of by their

sin. Though the sin by which especially they had made themselves thus miserable was their vile treatment of Him (for Jerusalem was a city that had been peculiarly injurious to Him), and though Christ knew how cruelly He would be treated in that city before that week was past, how He there would be set at nought, and with great malignity bound, falsely accused, condemned, reviled, spat upon, scourged, and crucified, yet all does not prevent His most affectionate tears of compassion towards them. "When He was come near, He beheld the city, and wept over it, saying, 'If thou hadst known, even thou (thou, as wicked as thou art, and as vile as thou hast been in thy treatment of Me; even thou), the things which belong unto thy peace! But now they are hid from thine eyes" (Luke 19:41–42; compare Matthew 23:37 and Luke 13:34). One would have thought He would have been more concerned for Himself than Jerusalem, as He had such a dreadful cup to drink, and was to suffer such extreme things by the cruelty of Jerusalem that week. But He, as it were, forgets His own sorrow and death, and weeps over the misery of His cruel enemies.

Ministers should imitate their great Master in His fervent prayers for the good of the souls of men. We find it to be Christ's manner, whenever He undertook anything of special importance in the work of His ministry, first to retire and pour out His soul in extraordinary prayer to His Father. Thus, when He was about to enter on a journey, and go on a circuit throughout all Galilee to preach in their synagogues, "He rose up a great while before day, and went out, and departed into a solitary place, and there prayed" (Mark 1:35). And when He was about to choose His twelve apostles, and send them out to preach the gospel, He first went out into a mountain to pray, and continued all night in prayer to God (Luke 6:12). And the night before His crucifixion, wherein He offered up Himself as a sacrifice for the souls of men, He poured out His soul in extraordinary prayer for those He was about to die for, as we have an account of in John 17. That wonderful and most affecting prayer of His was not so much for Himself as for His people. Although He knew what amazing sufferings He was to undergo the next day, yet He seemed, as it were, to be unmindful of Himself, and to have His heart all taken up with concern about His disciples. This He manifested in His spending so much time in comforting and counseling them, and praying for them with great affection, compassion, earnest care, and fatherly tenderness.

And the prayers that He made in the garden of Gethsemane, under the amazing view of the cup He was to drink the next day, seem to be intercessory, especially the last of the three prayers which He there made. While in agony He prayed more earnestly. His sweat was, as it were, great drops of blood falling down to the ground. He did not pray that the cup might pass from Him, as He had done before, but that God's will might be done (compare Luke 22:44 with Matthew 26:42). That prayer, as the Apostle teaches us (Hebrews 5:6–7), was a prayer that He put up as our High Priest, and therefore must be a prayer of intercession for us, a prayer offered up with His blood which He sweated in His agony—as prayers were wont to be offered up with blood of the sacrifices in the temple. His prayer at that time ("Thy will be done") was not only an expression of submission, but had the form of a petition, as it is in the Lord's Prayer. He prayed that God's will might be done in His being enabled to do the will of God, persevering in obedience unto death; and He prayed for the success of His sufferings, which might, in an eminent manner, be called the will of God, as it is in Psalm 40:7–8: "Then said I, 'Lo, I come; I delight to do Thy will, O My God."

Ministers should follow the example of Christ in His diligence and laboriousness in His work. "He went about doing good, and healing all that were oppressed of the devil" (Acts 10:38). So abundant was He in labors that oftentimes He scarcely allowed Himself time to eat or drink, insomuch that His friends sometimes went out to lay hold of Him, saying, "He is beside Himself" (Mark 3:20–21). Those three and a half years of His public ministry were so filled with action and labor that one of His disciples, who constantly attended Him, and who was an eyewitness of His activity, tells us that if all that He did should be written, the world would not contain the books.

Ministers should follow the example of Christ in His readiness not only to labor, but suffer for the salvation of souls, to spend and be spent for them. In this respect the apostle Paul imitated his Lord and Master. Philippians 2:17: "Yea, and if I be offered upon the sacrifice and service of your faith, I joy and rejoice with you all." Colossians 1:24: "Who now rejoice in my sufferings for you, and fill up that which is behind of the afflictions of Christ in my flesh, for His body's sake, which is the Church." 2 Corinthians 12:15: "And I will very gladly spend and be spent for you." Christ, in His prayers, labors, and sufferings for the souls of men is represented as travailing in birth with them. Isaiah 53:11: "He shall see of the travail of His soul." In like manner should ministers travail for the conversion and salvation of their hearers. They should imitate the faithfulness of Christ in His ministry, in speaking whatsoever God had commanded Him, and declaring the whole counsel of God. They should imitate Him in the manner of His preaching. He taught not as the scribes, but with authority, boldly, zealously, and fervently; insisting chiefly on the most important things in religion, being much in warning men of the danger of damnation, setting forth the greatness of the future misery of the ungodly; insisting not only on the outward, but also the inward and spiritual duties of religion; being much in declaring the great provocation and danger of spiritual pride and a self-righteous disposition, yet much insisting on the necessity and importance of inherent holiness and the practice of piety. He behaved Himself with admirable wisdom in all that He said and did in His ministry, amidst the many difficulties, enemies, and temptations He was surrounded with, wonderfully adapting His discourses to persons, seasons, and occasions. Isaiah 50:4: "The Lord God hath given Me the tongue of the learned, that I should know how to speak a word in season to him that is weary."

Ministers should follow their Master in His zeal, so wonderfully mixed and tempered with gentleness and condescension in His dealing with souls; preaching the gospel to the poor, and taking a gracious notice from time to time of little children. And they should imitate their Lord in His following the work of the ministry not from mercenary views, or for the sake of worldly advantages, but for God's glory and men's salvation; and in having His heart engaged in His work, it being His great delight and His meat to do the will of His Father and finish His work (John 4:34). He had His heart set on the success of His great undertaking in the salvation of souls. This was the joy that was set before Him, for which He ran His race, endured the cross, and despised the shame. His delight in the prospect of the eternal salvation of souls more than countervailed the dread He had of His extreme sufferings. Many waters could not quench His love, neither could the floods drown it, for His love was stronger than death, yea, than the mighty pains and torments of such a death.

II. I now proceed to the second thing proposed in the handling of this subject, which was to give some reasons why ministers of the gospel should follow the example of their great Lord and Master, Jesus Christ.

1. They should follow His example because He is their Lord and Master. Christ, as He is a divine person, is the Lord of heaven and earth, and so one of infinite dignity, to whom our supreme respect is due. And on that account He is infinitely worthy that we should regard not only His precepts, but His example. The infinite honorableness of His person recommends His virtues, and a conformity to them, as our greatest dignity and honor.

Christ is more especially the Lord of Christians, who are therefore under special obligations to follow Him. He is their Shepherd, and surely the flock should follow their shepherd. He is the Captain of their salvation, and it becomes soldiers to follow their captain and leader. He is their Head, not only their head of rule and authority, but their head of influence and communication, their vital head. Christians are members of His body; but members, as partakers of the life and spirit of the head, are conformed to the head.

But Christ is still in a more peculiar manner the Lord and Master of ministers of the gospel, as they are not only members of His Church, but the officers of His kingdom and the dignified servants of His family. It is the manner of a people to imitate their prince, but especially the ministers of his kingdom, and officers of his household. It is the duty of the whole army to follow their general, but especially of those officers who have a commission under him.

2. Ministers of the gospel are, in some respects, called and devoted to the same work and business to which Christ Himself was appointed. Ministers are not men's mediators, for there is but one Mediator between God and man, the man Christ Jesus. They are not our priests to make atonement and work out righteousness for us, for Christ, by one offering, has perfected forever those who are sanctified. They are not lords

over God's heritage, for one is their Master, even Christ. Yet ministers of the gospel, as Christ's servants and officers under Him, are appointed to promote the designs of that great work of Christ, the work of salvation. It is the work that ministers are devoted to, and therefore they are represented as co-workers with Christ. 2 Corinthians 6:1: "We then, as workers together with Him, beseech you also that ye receive not the grace of God in vain." Christ is the Savior of the souls of men; ministers also are spoken of in Scripture as saving men's souls. 1 Timothy 4:16: "In doing this, thou shalt both save thyself and them that hear thee." Romans 11:14: "If by any means I may provoke to emulation them which are my flesh, and might save some of them." 1 Corinthians 9:22: "That I might by all means save some." And where it is said in Obadiah 21 that "saviors shall come upon Mount Zion," ministers of the gospel are supposed to be there intended.

The work of ministers is in many respects like the work that Christ Himself was appointed to as the Savior of men, and especially the same as the work which Christ does in His prophetic office, only with this difference: that ministers are to speak and act wholly under Christ, as taught of Him, as holding forth His Word, and by light and strength communicated from Him. Christ Himself, after His baptism, followed the work of the ministry. He was a minister of the true sanctuary (Hebrews 8:2). He spoke and acted as His Father's minister. He was a minister of the gospel, and as such preached and administered sacraments.

Pastors of churches are ministers of the same gospel, but in their ministry they act as the ministers of Christ. Jesus Christ is the great Bishop of souls; ministers are also bishops under Him. Christ came into the world that He might be the light of the world; ministers are set to be lights unto the churches, and are also set to be the light of the world

(Matthew 5:14). Christ is the bright and morning star; ministers are stars in Christ's hand. Christ is the messenger of the covenant; ministers are called messengers of the Lord of hosts. Christ is His people's shepherd, the Good Shepherd, the Great Shepherd of His sheep. Ministers are also frequently called shepherds, and are directed to feed the flock of Christ which He purchased with His own blood.

Seeing therefore that the work that ministers are called and devoted to is no other than the work of Christ, or the work that Christ does, certainly they ought to do His work; which they do not do unless they imitate Him and do as He does, or as He has set them an example.

3. The example of Christ is most worthy of ministers' imitation. His example was perfect, without error, blemish, or defect. And therefore His example is worthy to be made our rule, and to be regarded and followed without exception, limitation, or reserve, unless it is in those things which He did that were proper to His peculiar office. Christ's virtue was not only perfect, but was exercised in those circumstances and under those trials that rendered His virtuous acts vastly the most amiable of any that ever appeared in any creature, whether man or angel. If we consider the perfection of the virtue that Christ exercised, His virtue exceeded that of the most eminent saints, more than the purest gold exceeds the meanest and foulest ore. And if we consider the manner of its exercise, the trials under which it was exercised, and the blessed fruits it has brought forth, His virtue exceeds that of all other perfectly innocent creatures, and even of the brightest angel, as the sun in its glory exceeds the stars.

And this example was set for us in our own nature, and so is especially fitted for our imitation. There was in the man Christ Jesus, who was one of us and dwelt among us, such exercises of virtue as befit our state and circumstances in the world, as those who dwell in frail flesh and blood, and as members of human society, and dwellers in such a world of sorrow and death.

And then these amiable exercises of virtue in Christ were exhibited chiefly in the things which He did in that work wherein ministers are called to act as co-workers with Him. The bright and glorious example of Christ that is set before us is chiefly in what He did during the three and a half years of His public ministry, and in the devotion, heavenly-mindedness, humility, patience, meekness, forgiveness, self-denial, and charity which He exercised in the labors and sufferings He went through for the good of the souls of men. Therefore His example is especially set for the imitation of those who are set apart, that they may make it the whole business of their lives to seek the same good of souls.

4. Ministers should follow that example of Christ which has been spoken of because if they are fit to be ministers, and are such as have any right to take that work upon themselves, Christ has set them this example in what He has done for their souls. "I have given you an example (says Christ in our text) that you should do as I have done to you." Ministers should be animated in this work by a great love to the souls of men, and should be ready to spend and be spent for them; for Christ loved them, and gave Himself for them. He loved them with a love stronger than death. They should have compassion for men under their spiritual miseries as Christ had pity on them. They should be much in prayer for the people of their flock, considering how Christ prayed and agonized for them in tears of blood. They should travail in birth with the souls who are committed to their care, seeing their own salvation is the fruit of the travail of Christ's soul. They should exercise a meek and condescending spirit to the mean, weak and poor, and should, as it were, wash the feet of Christ's dis-

ciples. They should consider how Christ condescended to them when they were wretched, miserable, poor, blind, and naked, and how He abased Himself to wash their feet.

The chief trials of Christ's virtue, and so its most bright and eminent exercises, were in the abasement, labor, and suffering that He was the subject of for our salvation. This certainly may well endear those virtues to us, and greatly engage us to imitate that example. So the things whereof this example consists were things by which we have infinite benefit, without which we should have been unspeakably miserable forever and ever, and by virtue of which we have the glorious privilege of the children of God, and have a full title to the crown of exceeding glory and pleasures forevermore at God's right hand.

III. I now proceed, as was proposed, in the third place to apply what has been said to myself, and others who are employed in this sacred work of the gospel ministry, and to such as are about to undertake it or are candidates for it, and particularly to him who is now to be solemnly set apart to this work in this place.

We are those to whom these things especially belong. We may hear Christ saying to us this day, "I have given you an example, that ye should do as I have done." For the words of Christ in the text were not only spoken to the twelve, but are also spoken unto us. We have now had represented to us, though in a very imperfect manner, the example that Christ has set, and what reasons there are that we, above all others, should imitate it.

It is not only our great duty, but will be our greatest honor, to imitate Christ and do the work that He has done, and so act as co-workers with Him.

There are two kinds of persons who are given to Christ,

and appointed and devoted of God to be His servants, to be employed with Christ, and under Him, in His great work of the salvation of the souls of men: angels and ministers. The angels are, all of them, even the most exalted of them, subjected of God the Father to our Redeemer, and given to Him as His servants, to be subservient to the great designs of His saving and glorifying His elect. Hebrews 1:14: "Are they not all ministering spirits, sent forth to minister for them who shall be heirs of salvation?" And doubtless they were created for this very end: God made them for His Son, to be subservient to Him in this great work, which seems to be the chief design of all God's works. And the employment of ministers of the gospel in this respect is like that of the glorious angels. The principalities and powers in heavenly places esteem it not any debasement, but their great honor, to be employed as Christ's ministers in this work; for therein they are employed as the ministers of God in the greatest and most honorable of all God's works, that work of God wherein His glory is chiefly displayed, and which His heart was chiefly upon from eternity. It is the honor of the Son of God Himself that He is appointed to this work. It was because God the Father infinitely loved His Son, and delighted to put honor upon Him, that He appointed Him to be the author of that glorious work of the salvation of men. And when we consider the greatness, importance, and excellency of it, we have reason to be astonished at the condescension of God, that He would ever improve mere creatures as co-workers and ministers of Christ in this affair; for "who is sufficient for these things?" (2 Corinthians 2:16). Who is fit or worthy? Who is equal to a work of such dignity and vast importance?

Especially have we reason to wonder that God will employ not only holy and glorious angels, but feeble, frail, sinful worms of the dust in this work, who need redemption themselves! And yet the honor that is put upon faithful ministers is, in some respects, greater than that of the angels. They seem to be that kind of servants who are the most dignified of the two. For Christ makes His angels to be ministering spirits unto them, unto the faithful ministers, and the angels are their angels—as faithful ministers of the gospel are not only ministers to the Church, but dignified members of the Church, that spouse of the King of glory, on whom the most glorious angels, the highest ministers in the court of heaven, are appointed to attend.

And then Christ seems especially to delight to carry on His work of the salvation of souls through the ministrations of men, who have that nature that Christ is united to, and who are of those sons of men with whom He had His delight before the world was made. So it is by the ministration of men that the Scriptures are given; they were the penmen of the Holy Bible, and by them the gospel is preached to the world. By them ordinances are administered, and through their ministrations especially souls are converted. When Christ Himself was employed in the work of the ministry, in the time of His humiliation, but few, comparatively, were brought home to Him directly by His ministrations. It pleased Christ to reserve this honor for His disciples and ministers after His ascension, to whom He promised that they should, in this respect, do greater works than He (John 14:12); and accordingly it was by their preaching that the Gentile world was converted and Satan's kingdom overthrown. Thus God delights to perfect praise out of the mouths of babes and sucklings, that He may still the enemy and the avenger.

It will be our great honor that we are called to this work of Christ, if therein we follow Him: for therein we shall be like the Son of God. But if we are unfaithful in this office, and do not imitate our Master, our offense will be heinous in proportion to the dignity of our office, and our final and everlasting disgrace and ignominy proportionably great. Then we, who in honor are exalted up to heaven, shall be cast down proportionably low in hell.

Let us further consider that our following the example of Christ in the work of the ministry is the way to enjoy the sensible joyful presence of Christ with us. The disciples had the comfort of Christ's presence and conversation by following Him and going where He went. When we cease to follow Him, He will go from us, and we shall soon lose sight of Him.

Our being conformed to Christ's example will also be the way for us to be conformed to Him, and partake with Him in His privileges. It is the way for us to have His joy fulfilled in us. Christ, in doing the work to which the Father appointed Him, obtained a glorious victory over His enemies, and, having spoiled principalities and powers, triumphed over them. If we imitate His example, it will be the way for us, in like manner, to conquer the principalities and powers, yea, to be much more than conquerors; it will be the way for us always to triumph in Jesus Christ. It will be the way for us to obtain success in our ministry, and actually to be made the happy instruments of the eternal salvation of souls. Christ has not only told us, but shown us the way to success in our business, and the way to victory over all who oppose us in it. And our imitating Christ in our ministry will be the way for us to be partakers with Him in His glory; the way for us in like manner to be approved, and openly honored and rewarded by God; the way to be brought to sit with Christ on His throne, as He is set down with the Father on His throne. And as Christ is now exalted to shine as the bright luminary and glory of heaven, so our following His example will be the way for us to be exalted, to shine with Him "as the stars forever and ever" (Daniel 12:3). And as Christ in heaven rejoices in His success, and will receive His Church, presented to Him without spot as His everlasting crown, so our imitating Christ in our work will be the way to partake with Christ in this joy, and have the souls whose salvation we are the instruments of to be our crown of rejoicing forever. Thus Christ and we shall rejoice together in that world of glory and joy where there is no more labor or sorrow. And we must enter into that joy and glory in the way of following Christ in our work; there is no other way for ministers to enter there.

And that we may thus follow Christ's example, and be partakers with Him in His glory, we need to be much in prayer for His Spirit. Christ Himself, though the eternal Son of God, obtained the Holy Spirit for Himself in a way of prayer. Luke 3:21–22: "Jesus being baptized, and praying, the heaven was opened, and the Holy Ghost descended like a dove upon Him." If we have the Spirit of Christ dwelling in us, we shall have Christ Himself thereby living in us, and then we shall undoubtedly live like Him. If that fountain of light dwells richly in us, we shall shine like Him, and so shall be burning and shining lights.

That we may be and behave like Christ, we should earnestly seek much acquaintance with Him, and much love for Him, and be much in secret converse with Him. It is natural, and, as it were, necessary, for us to imitate those whom we are much acquainted and conversant with, and have a strong affection for.

And in order for us to imitate Christ in the work of the ministry in any tolerable degree, we need not to have our hearts overcharged, and time filled up with worldly affections, cares, and pursuits. The duties of a minister that have been recommended are absolutely inconsistent with a mind much taken up with worldly profit, glory, amusements, and entertainments.

And another thing that is of very great importance in order for us to do the work that Christ did is that we take heed that the religion we promote be that same religion that Christ taught and promoted, and not any of its counterfeits and delusive appearances, or anything substituted by the subtle devices of Satan, or vain imaginations of men, in lieu of it. If we are zealous and very diligent to promote religion, but do not take good care to distinguish true from false religion, we shall be in danger of doing much more hurt than good with all our zeal and activity.

IV. I come now to the last thing proposed, to show what improvement should be made of what has been said by the people of this church and congregation, who are now about solemnly to commit their souls to the charge of him whom they have chosen to be their pastor, and who is now about to be set apart to that office.

And you, my brethren, as all of you have immortal souls to save, if you have considered the things that have been spoken, cannot but be sensible that it not only greatly concerns your elect pastor to take heed how he behaves himself in his great work, wherein he is to act as a co-worker with Christ for your salvation, but that it infinitely concerns you how you receive him and behave towards him. Seeing that it is for your eternal salvation that he is appointed to watch and labor, and seeing his business is to do the work of Christ for you, it is natural and easy to infer that your reception and entertainment of him should in some respect imitate the Church's reception of Jesus Christ. Galatians 4:14: "My temptation which was in my flesh, ye despised not, nor rejected; but received me as an angel of God, even as Christ Jesus."

Christ, in the text of this sermon, commands those whom He sends to follow His example. Then, in the 20th verse following, He directs those to whom He sends them how to treat them: "Verily, verily, I say unto you, he that receiveth whomsoever I send receiveth Me; and he that receiveth Me receiveth Him that sent Me." Seeing the work of your minister is in some respects the same as the work of Christ, and he is to be appointed and devoted to do this work for your souls in particular, surely you should esteem him very highly in love for his work's sake, do all that is in your power to help him, and put him under the best advantages to imitate his great Master in this work, to give himself wholly to his work, as Christ did during the time of His ministry, and to be successful in his work. And as it was observed before that it is impossible that ministers should in any tolerable degree imitate the example of Christ in their work if their minds are overcharged with worldly cares and concerns, you ought so to provide for him and support him that he shall have no need to entangle himself with these things. Otherwise you will not only bring a great temptation upon him which will vastly tend to hinder him in the work of Christ among you, but will, for the sake of sparing a little of your worldly substance for yourselves, foolishly and miserably starve your own souls and the souls of your children, and will but cheat yourselves; for you will not be in the way to prosper either in your spiritual or temporal concerns. The way to have your houses filled with plenty is to "honor the Lord with your substance, and with the first-fruits of all your increase" (Proverbs 3:9).

And as it is your duty and interest well to support your minister, so it concerns you to pray earnestly for him, and each one to do what in him lies in all respects to encourage and help him, and strengthen his hands by attending diligently to his ministry, receiving the truth in love, treating him with the honor due to a messenger of Christ, carefully avoiding all contention with him, and one with another. And take heed in particular that you do not forsake him to follow those who, under pretense of extraordinary purity, are doubtless doing the devil's work in separating themselves, and endeavoring to draw off others from the ministers and churches in the land in general.

If you think I have spoken something freely to you, I hope it will be considered that this is probably the last time you will ever hear me speak from the pulpit, and that I shall never see you again till we see one another in the invisible and eternal world where these things will open to us all in their just importance.

And now nothing is left but to express my sincerest wishes and prayers that the God of all grace would be with you and your elect pastor, and that He would give you in him a great and long-lasting blessing, that you may enjoy much of the presence of Christ with you in him; that in him may be made up the great loss you sustained by the death of your former faithful and eminent pastor, whose praise was in all the churches; and that you may receive him as you ought to receive a faithful minister of Jesus Christ. I pray that you may be a great comfort to him, and may receive great spiritual and eternal benefit by his means, and that you may be each other's crown of rejoicing in the day of the Lord Jesus.

Unbelievers Condemn the Glory and Excellency of Christ

"This is the stone which was set at nought of you builders."
Acts 4:11

In the foregoing chapters of Acts we have an account of the outpouring of the Holy Ghost on the Apostles, and of its extraordinary effects in their speaking boldly in the name of Jesus—speaking many strange languages, and so being made the instruments of the sudden conversion of vast multitudes. And in the chapter immediately preceding there is an account how Peter and John miraculously healed a man who had been a cripple from his birth, which, together with the word which they spoke to the people who flocked together on the occasion, was the means of a new access to the church. So the number of those who heard the Word and believed, as we are told in Acts 4:4, was about five thousand.

This sudden and extraordinary progress of the gospel greatly alarmed the priests and scribes, and other chief men among the Jews, so that they laid hands on Peter and John and put them in jail; and, the next day, brought them forth to appear before them, and called them to an account for what they had done. They asked them particularly by what power, or by what name, they had wrought the miracle on the impotent man. Upon this Peter, filled with the Holy Ghost, answered, "Ye rulers of the people, and elders of Israel, be it known unto you all, and to all the people of Israel, that by the name of Jesus Christ of Nazareth, whom ye crucified, whom God raised from the dead, even by Him doth this man stand

Unbelievers Condemn the Excellency of Christ

here before you whole. This is the stone which was set at nought of you builders, which is become the head of the corner." The Apostle quoted to them as now fulfilled Psalm 118:22: "The stone which the builders refused is become the head-stone of the corner." This text in that psalm the Apostle applied by telling them:

1. That "This is the stone," i.e., this person of whom he had spoken in the foregoing verse, Jesus Christ of Nazareth, whom they had crucified, and whom God had raised from the dead.

2. That they were the builders spoken of. They before whom the Apostle then was, and to whom he was speaking, were the rulers, elders, and scribes of the people, the high priest and other priests. They, as they were set to be rulers and teachers among God's people, by their office were called to be builders of the Church of God.

3. That they set this stone at nought. They had so done by refusing to accept Him. Christ came to His own, and His own received Him not; and not only so, but they had openly manifested the greatest contempt of Him. They had mocked Him, scourged and spat upon Him, and in derision crowned Him with a crown of thorns, arrayed Him in a mock robe, and then had put Him to a most ignominious death.

4. That notwithstanding this, He had become the head of the corner. In spite of all that they could do, He had obtained the chief place in the building. God had made Him the main foundation of it by raising Him from the dead, and so putting great honor upon Him; by pouring out His Spirit and enduing His disciples with extraordinary gifts; by suddenly converting so many thousands to be the followers of Christ. They put Him to death that He might have no followers, concluding that that would utterly put an end to His interest in Judea. But they were greatly disappointed, for the gospel had incompa-

rably greater success after Christ's death than before. God had accomplished the very thing which they endeavored to prevent by Christ's crucifixion: Christ's being believed in and submitted to as the great prophet of God and prince of His people.

DOCTRINE: Unbelievers set at nought the glory and excellency in Christ.

1. They set at nought the excellency of His person. Christ is a great and glorious person, a person of infinite worthiness, on which account He is infinitely esteemed and loved of the Father, and is continually adored by the angels. But unbelievers have no esteem at all for Him on that account. They have no value for Him on account of His being the Son of God. He is not set the higher in their esteem on the account of His standing in so near and honorable a relation to God the Father. He is not valued at all the more for His being a divine person. By His having the divine nature, He is infinitely exalted above all created beings. But He is not at all exalted by it in their esteem. They set nothing by His infinite majesty. His glorious brightness and greatness excite no true respect or reverence in them.

Christ is the Holy One of God. He is so holy that the heavens are not pure in His sight. He is possessed of all that holiness which is the infinite beauty and loveliness of the divine nature. But an unbeliever sets nothing by the holiness of Christ. Christ is the wisdom and power of God (1 Corinthians 1:24). But an unbeliever sets nothing by His power and wisdom. The Lord Jesus Christ is full of grace and mercy; the mercy and love of God appear nowhere else so brightly and gloriously as they do in the face of Jesus Christ. But an unbeliever sets no value at all upon the infinite grace of Christ.

Neither do unbelievers set anything by those excellent virtues which appeared in Christ's human nature when He was on earth. He was holy, harmless, undefiled, and separate from sinners. He was meek and lowly of heart. He was patient under afflictions and injuries; when He was reviled, He reviled not again. But unbelievers set nothing by these things in Jesus Christ. They very often hear how excellent and glorious a person Christ is. They are told of His holiness, grace, condescension, and meekness, and have the excellencies of Christ plainly set forth to them—yet they set all at nought.

2. They set at nought His excellency in His work and office. They are told how glorious and complete a mediator He is, how sufficient to answer all our necessities, and to save sinners to the uttermost; but they make light of it all. Yea, they make nothing of it. They hear of the wonderful wisdom of God in contriving such a way of salvation by Christ, they have the manifold wisdom of God set forth to them, but they make no account of the excellency of this way of salvation.

The unbeliever hears what a wonderful thing it was that He who was in the form of God, and esteemed it no robbery to be equal with God, should take upon Himself the human nature, and come and live in this world in a mean and low condition—but he makes nothing of this. He hears much of the dying love of Christ to sinners, how wonderful it was that so glorious a person, who is infinitely above the angels, should so set His love on such worms of the dust as to come and be made a curse for them, and die a cruel and ignominious death in their stead—but he sets nothing by all this. This dying love of Christ is of no account with him; those great things that Christ has done and suffered are, with him, light matters.

Unbelievers not only set little by the glory and excellency of Christ, but they set nothing by these things. Notwithstanding all the shows and pretenses which many natural men make of respect of Christ by speaking honorably of Him in their prayers, in their common conversation, and by coming to sacraments and attending other ordinances of Christ, yet indeed they do not set so much by all the glory and excellency of Christ—either of His person or His work as a Savior—as they do by the smallest earthly enjoyment.

I proceed now to mention some evidences of the truth of this doctrine.

1. They never give Christ any honor on account of His glory and excellency. They may, and often do, pay Christ an external and seeming respect, but they do not honor Him in their hearts. They have no exalting thoughts of Christ, no inward respect or reverence towards Him. All their outward worship is only feigned; none of it arises from any real honor or respect in their hearts towards Christ. It is either only for fashion's sake, and in compliance with custom, or else it is forced and what they are driven to by fear, as we read Psalm 66:3: "Through the greatness of Thy power shall Thine enemies submit themselves unto Thee." In the original it is "shall Thine enemies lie unto Thee," i.e., yield a feigned obedience. Through the greatness of Christ's power, and for fear of His wrath, His enemies, who have no respect or honor for Him in their hearts, will lie to Him, and make a show of respect when they have none.

An unbeliever is not sensible that Christ is worthy of any glory, and therefore does not at all seek the glory of Christ in anything that he does. He does nothing in religion out of respect to Christ's glory, but wholly for other ends—which shows that he sees not Christ to be worthy of any glory. Christ is set last and lowest in the heart of an unbeliever. He has high thoughts of other things: he has high thoughts of created objects and earthly enjoyments, but mean and low thoughts of Christ.

The unbeliever shows the mean and contemptible

thoughts that he has of Christ in refusing to accept Him, and in shutting the door of his heart against Him. Christ stands at the door and knocks, and sometimes stands many years knocking at the door of his heart, but he refuses to open to Him. Now it certainly shows that men have a very mean thought of a person when they shut him out of their doors. Unbelievers show the mean and dishonorable thoughts they have of Christ in that they dare not trust Him. They believe not what He says to be true. They will not trust the word of Christ as far as the word of one of their honest neighbors, or of a servant whom they have found to be faithful. It also appears that they have no real honor for Christ in their hearts in that they refuse to obey His commands. They do nothing from a spirit of obedience to Him; that external obedience which they render is but a forced, feigned obedience, and not from any respect to Christ's authority or worthiness to be obeyed.

2. They have no love to Him on account of His glory and excellency. If they saw any excellency in Christ, they would have some measure of love to Him. But the truth is, they see no form or comeliness in Christ, and hence they have no love at all to Him. An unbeliever never exercises one act of true love to Christ. All that he is told of His divine perfections, of His holiness, His meekness and grace, has no influence at all to draw forth any love. The display of these things no more draws forth love out of the heart of an unbeliever than it draws forth love from the stones and rocks.

A natural man has no love of benevolence towards Christ. Notwithstanding all that is declared to him of the excellency of Christ, he has no goodwill towards Him. He rejoices not in His glory and happiness; he would not care what became of Christ if he could but escape hell. If Christ should be dethroned, or should cease to be, he has not so much good will toward Christ as would make him concerned about it. And if the kingdom and interest of Christ in the world should go to ruin, it would be in no way grievous to the unbeliever, provided his own interest could be secure.

So also an unbeliever has no love of complacency in Jesus Christ for His excellency. He takes no delight in the consideration of that excellency of Christ of which he is told. He is told that it is exceedingly beautiful and glorious, but the thoughts of the glory of Christ are in no way entertaining to him. He has no delight in the thoughts of it, or in any comtemplations upon it. He takes delight in thinking of earthly objects; but when he comes to turn his mind upon Jesus Christ, if ever he so does, this is to him a dry and barren subject. He finds nothing there to feed and delight his soul, no beauty or loveliness to please or gratify him.

3. Unbelievers have no desires after the enjoyment of Christ. If they set anything by the excellency of Christ, they would have some desires after Him on account of that excellency—especially when He is offered to them, and is from time to time set forth as the proper object of their choice and desires. That which men prize they are wont to desire, especially if it is represented to them as attainable, and as fit and suitable for them. But unbelievers only desire to be delivered from hell, not to enjoy Christ.

They cannot conceive what happiness there can be in beholding Christ and being with Him, in seeing His holiness, and in contemplating His wonderful grace and divine glory. They have no relish for any such thing, nor appetite after it.

4. They show that they set at nought the glory and excellency of Christ in that they seek not a conformity to that glory and excellency. A natural man may seek to be holy, but it is not for holiness' sake; it is only that he may escape wrath. He has no desires after holiness, nor is it indeed holiness that he

seeks, because he is all the while an enemy to holiness. A natural man has no desires to have his soul conformed to the glorious beauty and excellency of Christ, nor to have His image upon him.

If he prized or delighted in the excellencies of Christ, he would necessarily desire to be like Him so far as he could. This we see in ourselves and in all men: when we see any qualifications in others that are pleasing to us, it is natural for us to endeavor to imitate and be conformed to those persons. Hence men are apt to learn of those for whom they have a great esteem. They naturally fall into an imitation of their ways and manner of behavior. But natural men feel within themselves no disposition or inclination to learn of Christ or imitate Him. Their tempers and dispositions remain quite contrary to Christ's; neither do they grow at all better or more conformed to Him, but rather worse. 2 Timothy 3:13: "Evil men and seducers shall wax worse and worse."

Application

1. This doctrine may teach us the heinousness of the sin of unbelief, as this sin sets all the glory and excellency of Christ at nought. It often appears strange to natural men that unbelief should be spoken of as such a heinous and crying sin. They cannot see such evil in it. There are other sins which often trouble their consciences while this troubles them not at all, though it is that which brings far greater guilt upon them than those sins about which they are more troubled.

What has been said may show why unbelief is spoken of as a heinous sin (John 3:18, 16:9 and 1 John 5:10). For thereby all the glory of Christ is set at nought, though it is so great, though it is infinite, though it is the glory of the Godhead itself, and though it has been so gloriously manifested in what

Christ has done and suffered. Natural men, in their unbelief, cast contempt on all this glory, and tread it under foot as being worth nothing. Their unbelief treats the excellency of Christ as being of less value than the meanest earthly enjoyments.

2. This doctrine may convict natural men in four particulars:

(1) Hereby you may be convinced of the greatness of your guilt. Consider how great and excellent that Person is whom you thus set at nought. Contempt of any person is heinous in proportion to the worthiness and dignity of the person condemned. Though we are but worms of the dust, and very vile, sinful creatures, yet we take it grievously when we are despised. Consider how you yourselves are ready to resent it when any of your neighbors seem to slight you, and set light by what you say and do, and to make no account of it, but to treat you as if you were good for nothing, or not worth minding. Do you take this well of your neighbors and equals when you observe anything of this nature? Are you not ready to look upon it with resentment, to think very ill of it, and to judge that you have great cause to be offended?

But if it is such a crime to despise you and set you at nought, what is it to set at nought the eternal, infinitely glorious Son of God, in comparison with whom you and all nations are nothing, and less then nothing, and vanity? You dislike it much to be condemned by your equals, but you would take it yet more grievously to be despised by your inferiors, by those whom, on every account, you must exceed. What a crime is it, then, for a vile, sinful worm to set at nought Him who is the brightness of the glory of the King of kings!

It would be a crime inexpressibly heinous to set little by the glory and excellency of such a person; but it is more so to set nothing at all by it, as you do. You have no value at all for

Unbelievers Condemn the Excellency of Christ

it, as has been shown. And this is the more aggravated since Christ is a person whom you so much need, and since He came into the world, out of infinite grace to sinners, to lay down His life to deliver them from hell, and purchase for them eternal glory. How much has Christ done and suffered that you might have opportunity to be saved! Yet you set nothing by the blood of Christ, even that blood that was shed for such poor sinners as you are, and that is offered to you for your salvation. But you trample under foot the blood of the Son of God. If Christ had come into the world only to teach us, it would have been a heinous thing to trample under foot His Word and instructions. But when He came to die for us, how much more heinous is it to trample under foot His blood!

Men take it hard to have any of their qualifications or actions despised which they esteem commendable. But especially do they highly resent it when others slight their kindness. And above all when they put themselves out of their way, and have denied themselves, and suffered considerably to do others a kindness; *then* to have their kindness despised and set at nought is what men would above all things resent. How heinous then is it, and how exceedingly provoking to God must it be, thus to set at nought so great kindness and love of Christ, when from love to sinners He suffered so much!

Consider how highly the angels, who are so much above you, regard the glory and excellency of Christ. They admire and adore the glory of Christ, and cease not day nor night to praise the same in the most exalted strains. Revelation 5:11-12: "And I beheld, and I heard the voice of many angels round about the throne and the beasts and the elders; and the number of them was ten thousand times ten thousand, and thousands of thousands, saying with a loud voice, 'Worthy is the Lamb that was slain, to receive power, and riches, and wisdom, and strength, and honor, and glory, and blessing.' " The saints admire the excellency of Christ, the glorious angels admire it, and every creature in heaven and earth, except you unbelieving children of men.

Consider not only how much the angels set by the glory of Christ, but how much God Himself sets by it; for He is the darling of heaven. He was eternally God's delight, and because of His glory God has thought Him worthy to be appointed the heir of all things, and has seen fit to ordain that all men should honor the Son even as they honor the Father. Is He thus worthy of the infinite esteem and love of God Himself? And is He worthy of no esteem from you?

(2) Hereby you may be convinced of your danger. You must know that such guilt will bring great wrath. Dreadful destruction is denounced in Scripture against those who despise only the disciples of Christ (Matthew 18:6). What destruction, then, will come on those who despise all the glorious excellency of Christ Himself?

Consider that you not only have no value for all the glory and excellency of Christ, but you are enemies to Him on that very account. The very ground of that enmity and opposition which there is between your hearts and Jesus Christ is the glorious perfections and excellencies that there are in Jesus Christ. By being such a holy and excellent Savior, He is contrary to your lusts and corruptions. If there were a Savior offered to you that was agreeable to your corrupt nature, such a Savior you would accept. But Christ being a Savior of such purity, holiness, and divine perfection, this is the cause why you have no inclination to Him, but are offended in Him.

Instead of being a precious stone in your eyes, He is a stone of stumbling and a rock of offense to you. That He is a Savior who has manifested such divine perfections in what He has done and suffered is one principal reason why you set nothing by Him. Consider how provoking this must be to God the Father, who has given His only-begotten Son for your salvation, and what wrath it merits from the Son whom you thus treat. And consider how you will hereafter bear this wrath.

Consider that however Christ is set at nought by you, He shall be the head of the corner. Though you set Him low, yet He shall be exalted even with respect to you. It is but a vain thing for you to make light of Christ and treat Him with contempt. However much you condemn Him, you cannot break His bands asunder nor cast His cords from you. You will still be in His hands. While you despise Christ, God will despise you, and the Lord will have you in derision. God will set His King on His holy hill of Zion in spite of all His enemies (Psalm 2:1–6). Though you say, "We will not have this man to reign over us," yet Christ will rule over you. Psalm 110:2: "Rule Thou in the midst of Thine enemies." If you will not submit to the scepter of His grace, you shall be subject to the rod of His wrath, and He will rule you with a rod of iron (Psalm 2:9–12).

(3) You may hence be led to see how worthless many of those things in yourselves are that you have been ready to make much of. Particularly, if you set nothing by all the glory of Christ, what are those desires that you have after Christ good for? And what is that willingness that you think you find to come to Christ? Sinners are often wont to excuse themselves in their unbelief because they see not but that they are willing to come to Christ, and would gladly come to Him if they could. And they make much of such desires, as though God were unjust to punish them for not coming to Christ when they would gladly come if they could. But this doctrine shows that your willingness and desires to come to Christ are not worthy to be mentioned as any excuse; for they are not from any respect to Christ, but are merely forced. You at the same time set nothing by all His excellency and glory.

So you may hence learn the worthlessness of all your pains and endeavors after Christ. When sinners have taken a great deal of pains to get an interest in Christ, they are wont to make a righteousness of it—little considering that, at the very time they are taking so much pains, they set nothing at all by Christ for any glory or excellency there is in Him, but set Him wholly at nought, and seek Him out of respect to their own interest.

(4) Hence learn how justly God might forever refuse to give you an interest in Christ. For why should God give you any part or interest in Him whom you set at nought, all whose glory and excellency you value not in the least, but rather trample it under your feet?

Why should God give you any interest in Him whom you so despise? Seeing you despise Him, how justly might you be obliged to go without any interest in Him! How justly might you be refused any part in that precious stone whose preciousness you esteem no more than that of the stones in the street! Is God obliged to cast such a pearl before swine who will trample it under their feet? Is God obliged to make you possessors of His infinitely glorious and dear Son when, at the same time, you count Him not worth having for the sake of any worth or excellency that there is in Him, but merely because you cannot escape hell without Him?

Praise One of the Chief Employments of Heaven

"And I heard a voice from heaven, as the voice of many waters, and as the voice of a great thunder; and I heard the voice of harpers harping with their harps." Revelation 14:2

We may observe in these words:
1. What it was that John heard: the voice and melody of a company praising God. It is said in the next verse that they sang a new song before the throne.
2. Whence he heard this voice: "I heard a voice from heaven." This company that he heard praising God was in heaven. It is said in the following verse: "They sang this song before the throne, and before the four living creatures, and the elders." But the throne of God, the four living creatures, and the four and twenty elders are all represented in these visions of John as being in heaven. So this voice was the voice of the heavenly inhabitants, the voice of the blessed and glorious company that is in heaven before the throne of God there.
3. The kind of voice: which is here set forth in a very lively and elegant manner. It is said to be as the voice of many waters, as the voice of mighty thunders, and as the voice of harpers harping with their harps.
Hereby several things are represented in a very striking manner:
The distance of the voice: it was the voice of a vast and innumerable multitude, so that it was "as the voice of many waters." How naturally this represents the joint, continual, and loud voice of a vast multitude at a distance, that it

resembled the voice of many waters.

The loudness of the voice. It was as the voice of many waters and as the voice of a great thunder, which describes the extraordinary fervency of their praises, and how lively and vigorous they were therein, and how everyone praised God with all his might. They all, joining together, sang with such fervency that heaven, as it were, rang with their praises. The noise of thunder and the roaring of many waters are the greatest and most majestic sounds ever heard upon earth, and are often spoken of in the Scriptures as the mightiest sounds. John could not distinctly hear what they said, but they, being in heaven, at a great distance, he knew not what better to compare it to than to the roaring of the sea, or a great thunder.

Yet it was a melodious sound, signified by this expression: "I heard the voice of harpers harping with their harps." The harp was a stringed instrument that David made much use of in praising God. John represents the matter thus to us: that the voice which he heard, being at a great distance, was indistinct. It was of such a vast multitude, and such a mighty, fervent voice, that it seemed in some measure like distant thunder or the roaring of water; and yet he could perceive the music of the voice at the same time. Though it was, in some respects, as thunder and the noise of water, yet there was a sweet and excellent melody in it. In short, though these comparisons of which John makes use to signify to us what kind of a voice and sound it was that he heard are exceedingly lively and elegant, yet it seems to be evident from them that what he heard was inexpressible, and that he could find nothing that could perfectly represent it. That a voice should be as the voice of many waters and as the voice of a great thunder, and yet like the voice of harpers, is to us not easily to be conceived of. But the case was that John could find no earthly sound that was sufficient to represent it; and therefore such various and different similitudes are aggregated and cast together to represent it. But this much seems to be signified by it: it seemed to be the voice of an innumerable multitude, and they were exceedingly fervent and mighty in their praises. The voice of this multitude was very great, and exceedingly full of majesty, and yet a most sweet and melodious voice at the same time.

DOCTRINE: The work of the saints in heaven very much consists in praising God.

PROPOSITION 1. The saints in heaven are employed; they are not idle. They have there much to do; they have a work before them that will fill up eternity.

We are not to suppose that when the saints have finished their course and done the works appointed them here in this world, and have gotten to their journey's end, to their Father's house, they will have nothing to do. It is true that the saints, when they get to heaven, rest from their labors and their works follow them. Heaven is not a place of labor and travail, but a place of rest. Hebrews 4:9: "There remains a rest for the people of God." And it is a place of the reward of labor. But yet the rest of heaven does not consist in idleness and cessation of all action, but only a cessation from all the trouble, toil and tediousness of action. The most perfect rest is consistent with being continually employed. So it is in heaven. Though the saints are exceedingly full of action, yet their activity is perfectly free from all labor, weariness, or unpleasantness. They shall rest from their work, that is, from all work of labor, self-denial, grief, care, and watchfulness; but they will not cease from action. The saints in glory are represented as employed in serving God as well as the saints on earth, though it is without any difficulty or opposition. Revelation 22:3: "And there shall be no more curse; but the throne of God and of the Lamb shall be in it, and His servants shall serve Him." Yea, we are told that they shall serve God day and night, that is, continually or without ceasing. Revelation 7:15: "Therefore are they before the throne of God, and serve Him day and night in His temple." And yet this shall be without any manner of trouble, as follows in the next verse: "They shall hunger no more, neither thirst any more, neither shall the sun light on them nor any heat." In this world saints labor, as it were, in the wearisome heat of the sun; but there, though they shall still serve God, yet shall the sun not light on them, nor shall any heat. In one sense, the saints and angels in heaven rest not day nor night (Revelation 4:8), that is, they never cease from their blessed employment. Perfection of happiness does not consist in idleness, but, on the contrary, it very much consists in action. The angels are blessed spirits, and yet they are exceedingly active in serving God. They are as a flame of fire, which is the most active thing that we see in this world. God Himself enjoys infinite happiness and perfect bliss, and yet He is not inactive, but is Himself, in His own nature, a perfect act, and is continually at work in bringing to pass His own purposes and ends. That principle of holiness that is in its perfection in the saints in heaven is a most active principle; so that though they enjoy perfect rest, yet they are a great deal more active than they were when in this world. In this world they were exceedingly dull, heavy, and inactive; but now they are a flame of fire. The saints in heaven are not merely passive in their happiness. They do not merely enjoy God passively, but in an active manner. They are not only acted upon by God, but they mutually act towards Him; and in this action and reaction consists the heavenly happiness.

PROPOSITION 2. Their employment consists very much in praising God.

John, the beloved disciple, often had visions of heaven, and in almost every instance had a vision of the inhabitants as praising God. So in Revelation 4 he tells us that he looked, and behold, a door was opened in heaven, and he was called up thither, and that he saw the throne of God and Him who sat on the throne. And then he gives us an account of how those who were round about the throne were praising God: "the four living creatures rest not day nor night, saying, 'Holy, holy, holy Lord God Almighty, which was and is and is to come.' And when those living creatures give glory and honor and thanks to Him, the four and twenty elders fall down before Him and worship Him."

Again in Revelation 5:8–9, we have an account of how they sing praises to Christ. And so in Revelation 7:9–12; 11:16–17; 12:10; and 15:2–4. And in the beginning of the nineteenth chapter we have an account of how the hosts of heaven sing hallelujahs to God. By all this it most evidently appears that their work very much consists in praising God and Christ. We have but a very imperfect knowledge of the future state of blessedness and of their employment; without a doubt they have various employments there. We cannot reasonably question but they are employed in contributing to each other's delight. They shall dwell together in society. They shall also probably be employed in contemplating God, His glorious perfections and glorious works, and so gaining knowledge in these things. And doubtless they will be employed in many ways that we know nothing of; but this we may determine: that much of their employment consists in praising God, and that for the following reasons.

1. Because there they see God. This is the blessedness promised to the saints, that they shall see God (Matthew 5:8). They who see God cannot *but* praise Him. He is a Being of such glory and excellence that the sight of this excellence of

His will necessarily influence those who behold it to praise Him. Such a glorious sight will awaken and rouse all the powers of the soul, and will irresistibly impel and draw them into acts of praise. Such a sight enlarges their souls and fills them with admiration, and with an unspeakable exultation of spirit.

It is from the little that the saints have seen of God, and know of Him in this world, that they are excited to praise Him in the degree they do here. But here they see but as in a glass darkly; they have only now and then a little glimpse of God's excellency; but then they shall have the transcendent glory and divine excellency of God set in their immediate and full view. They shall dwell in His immediate, glorious presence, and shall see face to face (1 Corinthians 13:12). Now the saints see the glory of God but by a reflected light, as we in the night see the light of the sun reflected from the moon; but in heaven they shall directly behold the Sun of righteousness, and shall look full upon Him when shining in all His glory. This being the case, it can be no otherwise but that they should very much employ themselves in praising God. When they behold the glorious power of God, they cannot but praise that power; when they see God's wisdom that is so wonderful, and infinitely beyond all created wisdom, they cannot but continually praise that wisdom; when they view the infinitely pure and lovely holiness of God, whereby the heavens themselves are not pure in comparison with Him, how can they avoid praising with an exalted heart that beauty of the divine nature! When they see the infinite grace of God, and see what a boundless ocean of mercy and love His is, how can they but celebrate that grace with the highest praise!

2. They will have another sense of the greatness of the fruits of God's mercy than we have here in this world. They will not only have a sight of the glorious attributes of God's goodness and mercy in their beatific vision of God, but they

will be sensible of the exceeding greatness of the fruits of it, the greatness of the benefits that He has bestowed. They will have another sense of the greatness and manifoldness of the communications of His goodness to His creation in general. They will be more sensible of how God is the fountain of all good, the Father of lights, from whom proceeds every good and perfect gift. We now but little consider, in comparison with what we should do, how full the world is of God's goodness, and how it appears in the sun, moon, and stars, and in the earth and seas, with all their fullness, and wheresoever we turn our eyes, and how all ranks and orders of being, from the highest angel to the lowest insect, are dependent upon, and maintained by, the goodness of God. These the saints in heaven clearly see: they see how the universe is replenished with His goodness, and how the communications of His goodness are incessantly issuing from God as from an ever-flowing fountain, and are poured forth all around in vast profusion into every part of heaven and earth, as light is every moment diffused from the sun. We have but faint, imperfect notions of these things, but the saints in heaven see them with perfect clearness. They have another sense of the greatness of God's goodness to mankind, to the Church, and to them in particular, than any of us have. They have another sense of the greatness of God's goodness in temporal mercies which God bestowed upon them while they were here in this world, though they know that spiritual mercies are infinitely greater. But especially they have an immensely greater sense of the exceeding greatness of the fruits of God's grace and mercy bestowed in redemption. They have another sense how great a gift the gift of God's only-begotten Son is. They have another sense of the greatness and dignity of the person of Christ, and how great a thing it was for Him to become man, and how great a thing it was for Him to lay down His life and endure the shameful and accursed death of the cross. They have another sense of how great the benefits are that Christ has purchased for men; how great a mercy it is to have sin pardoned, and to be delivered from the misery of hell. They have another sense of how dreadful that misery is, for the damned are tormented in the presence of the holy angels and saints, and they see the smoke of their torment; and they have another sense of what eternity is, and so are proportionably more sensible how great a mercy it is to be delivered from that torment. They have another sense of how great a fruit of God's grace it is to be the children of God, and to have a right and title to eternal glory. They are sensible of the greatness of the benefits that Christ has purchased by their experience, for they are in possession of that blessedness and glory that He has purchased; they taste the sweetness of it, and therefore they are more sensible of what cause they have to praise God for these things.

The grace and goodness of God in the work of redemption appear so wonderful to them that their thoughts of it excite them to the most ardent praise. When they take a view of the grace of God, and of the love of Christ in redemption, they see that there is cause that they should exert the utmost of their capacities, and spend an eternity in praising God and the Lamb. It is but a very little that we at best can conceive of the greatness of the benefits of redemption, and therefore we are but little affected by it, and our praises for it are low and dull things.

3. Another reason is that they will be perfect in humility. In order for a person to be rightly disposed to the work of praise, he must be a humble person. A proud person is for assuming all praise to himself, and is not disposed to ascribe it to God. It is humility only that will enable us to say from the heart, "Not unto us, not unto us, O Lord, but unto Thy name

be the glory." The humble person admires the goodness and grace of God to him. He sees more how wonderful it is that God should take such notice of him, and show such kindness to him, who is so much below His notice. Now the saints in heaven have this grace of humility perfected in them. They as much excel the saints on earth in humility as in other graces. Though they are so much above the saints on earth in holiness and in their exalted state, yet they are vastly more humble than the saints on earth are. They are as much lower in humility as they are higher in honor and happiness. And the reason for it is that they know more of God: they see more of His greatness and infinite highness, and therefore are so much the more sensible of their own comparative nothingness.

They are the more sensible of the infinite difference there is between God and them, and therefore are more sensible how wonderful it is that God should take so much notice of them as to have such communion with them, and give them such a full enjoyment of Himself. They are far more sensible of what unworthy creatures they have been, that God should bestow such mercies upon them more than the saints on earth.

They have a greater sight of the evil of sin. They see more what filthy, vile creatures they were by nature, and how dreadfully they provoked God by actual sin, and how they have deserved God's hatred and wrath. The saints in heaven have as much greater a sense of their unworthiness in their natural state than the saints on earth as they have a greater sense of God's glorious excellency; for it is the sight of God's excellency which gives them a sight of their own unworthiness. And therefore they proportionally admire the love of God to them in giving Christ to die for them, and the love of Christ in being willing to offer Himself for their sins, and of the wonderful mercy of God in their conversion, and bestowing eternal life upon them. The humble sense the saints have of their own unworthiness greatly engages and enlarges their hearts in praise to Him for His infinite mercy and grace.

4. Their love to God and Christ will be perfect. Love is a principal ingredient in the grace of thankfulness. There is a counterfeit thankfulness in which there is no love. But there is love in exercise in all sincere thankfulness. And the greater any person's love is, the more will he be disposed to praise. Love will cause him to delight in the work. He who loves God proportionably seeks the glory of God, and loves to give Him glory. Now the hearts of the saints in heaven are all, as it were, a pure flame of love. Love is the grace that never fails: where there are prophecies, they shall fail; where there is knowledge, it shall vanish away. Faith shall cease in vision, and hope in fruition, but love never fails. The grace of love will be exalted to its greatest height and highest perfection in heaven; and love will vent itself in praise. Heaven will ring with praise because it is full of love to God. This is the reason why that great assembly, that innumerable host, praises God with such ardency, that their praise is as the voice of many waters, and as the mighty thunderings, because they are animated by so ardent, vigorous, and powerful a principle of divine love.

Application

USE OF INSTRUCTION:
1. Hence we may learn the excellency of this work of praising God. That it is a most excellent employment appears because it is a heavenly employment. It is that work wherein the saints and angels are continually employed. If we sincerely and frequently praise God, we shall therein be like the heav-

enly inhabitants, and join with them.

That it is the work of heaven shows it to be the most honorable work. No employment can be a greater honor to a man than to praise God. It is the peculiar dignity of the nature of man, and the very thing wherein his nature is exalted above things without reason and things without life, that he is made capable of actively glorifying his Creator. Other creatures glorify God: the sun, moon, stars, the earth and waters, all the trees of the field, grass and herbs, and fishes and insects glorify God (Psalm 19:1–6; Job 12:7–8). But herein is the peculiar dignity of the nature of man, that he is capable of glorifying Him as a cause, by counsel, understandingly and voluntarily, which is a heavenly work.

2. This doctrine may give us an idea of the glorious and happy state of the saints in heaven. It shows how joyfully and gloriously they spend their time. Joy is a great ingredient in praise. There is an exultation of spirit in fervent praise. Praise is the most joyful work in the world. And how joyful a society are they who join together, so many thousands and millions of them, with one heart and one soul to sing a new song before the throne, who fill heaven with their glorious melody! How joyful they are in their work appears in the text by their fervency in it, so that their voices resounded as the voice of many waters, and as the voice of a great thunder. What ineffable joy was there in those harpers whom John heard harping with their harps!

This shows how different a state the saints in heaven are in from what they were in this world. Here much of the work to which the saints are called consists in laboring, in fighting, in toilsome traveling in a howling wilderness, in mourning and suffering, and in offering up strong crying and tears. But there in heaven their work continually is to lift up their joyful songs of praise.

This world is a valley of tears, a world filled with sighs and groans. One is groaning under some bodily pain; another is mourning and lamenting over a dear departed friend; another is crying out by reason of the arm of the oppressor. But in heaven there is no mixture of such sounds as these; there is nothing to be heard among them but the sweet and glorious melody of God's praises. There is a holy cheerfulness to be seen throughout that blessed society. Revelation 21:4: "And God shall wipe away all tears from their eyes, and there shall be no more death, neither sorrow nor crying." They shall never have anything more to do with sighing and crying; but their eternal work henceforward shall be praise.

This should make us long for heaven, where they spend their time so joyfully and gloriously. The saints especially have reason to be earnestly breathing after that happy state where they may in so joyful a manner praise God.

3. This may put natural persons upon reflecting on their own state, that they have no part nor lot in this matter. You are an alien from the commonwealth of Israel. You are not one of the people of God. You do not belong to their society who are to spend their eternity after that joyful manner which you have now heard. You have no right nor portion in heaven. If you hereafter come and offer yourself to be admitted into this blessed society in your present state, if you come and try to be admitted, you will be thrust out; you will be driven away. If you come and knock and cry to be admitted to the wedding, saying, "Lord, Lord, open unto us," all will be to no purpose! You will hear no other word except, "Depart!" You shall be shut out into outer darkness. You shall not be permitted to sing among the children, but shall be driven out to howl among dogs. Revelation 22:14–15: "Blessed are they that do His commandments, that they may have a right to the tree of life, and may enter in through the gates into the city;

for without are dogs." You are in danger of spending eternity not in joyfully singing praises, but in a quite contrary manner: in weeping, wailing, and gnashing of teeth, blaspheming God because of your pains and because of your plagues. You shall see others coming from the east and the west, sitting down with Abraham, Isaac, and Jacob in the kingdom of God, taking their places among that blessed, happy society, joining their voices in their heavenly music. But you see your lot; you shall have other work to do. Isaiah 65:14: "Behold, My servants shall sing for joy of heart; but ye shall cry for sorrow of heart, and howl for vexation of spirit."

USE OF EXHORTATION:
If it is so that praising God is very much the employment of heaven, hence let all be exhorted to the work and duty of praising God. The following considerations will show why we should be stirred up by this doctrine to this work:

1. Let it be considered that the Church on earth is the same society with those saints who are praising God in heaven. There is not one church of Christ in heaven and another here upon earth. Though the one is sometimes called "the church triumphant," and the other "the church militant," yet they are not indeed two churches. By "the church triumphant" is meant the triumphant part of the Church, and by "the church militant" the militant part of it; for there is but one universal or catholic Church. Song of Solomon 6:9: "My dove, my undefiled, is but one." Christ has not two mystical bodies. 1 Corinthians 12:12: "The body is one, and hath many members." The glorious assembly and the saints on earth make but one family. Ephesians 3:15: "Of whom the whole family in heaven and earth is named." Though some are in heaven and some on earth, in very different circumstances, yet they are all united; for there is "but one body and one

spirit, and one Lord Jesus Christ. One God and Father of all, who is above all, and through all, and in all." God has in Christ united the inhabitants of heaven and the holy inhabitants of this earth, and has made them one. Ephesians 1:10: "That in the dispensation of the fullness of times, He might gather together in one all things in Christ, both which are in heaven and which are on earth, even in Him." Heaven is a great distance from the earth; it is called a far country (Matthew 25:14). Yet the distance of place does not separate them so as to make two societies. For though the saints on earth at present are at a distance from heaven, yet they belong there; that is their proper home. The saints who are in this world are strangers here; and therefore the Apostle reproved the Christians in his day for acting as though they belonged to this world. Colossians 2:20: "Why, as though living in the world, are ye subject to ordinances?"

Some of a people may be in their own land, and some in a strange land, and yet be but one people. Some of a family may be at home, and some sojourning abroad, and yet be but one family. The saints on earth, though they are not actually in heaven, yet have their inheritance in heaven and are traveling towards heaven, and will arrive there in a little time. They are nearly related to the saints in heaven; they are their brethren, being children of the same Father and fellow heirs with Jesus Christ. In Ephesians 2:19, the saints on earth are said to be fellow citizens with the saints, and of the household of God. And the Apostle tells the Hebrew Christians (Hebrews 12:22–24) that they were "come to Mount Zion, and to the city of the living God, the heavenly Jerusalem, and to an innumerable company of angels, to the general assembly and church of the firstborn, which are written in heaven, and to God the Judge of all, and to the spirits of just men made perfect." But how were they come to this heavenly city and this glorious assembly when they were yet here on earth? They were come to them ere they were brought and united to them in the same family. But this is what I would inculcate by all this: that the Church of God on earth ought to be employed in the same work with the saints in heaven, because they are the same society. As they are but one family, and have but one Father and one inheritance, so they should have but one work. The Church on earth ought to join with the saints in heaven in their employment, as God has joined them in one society by His grace.

We profess to be of the visible people of Christ, to be Christians and not heathens, and so to belong to the universal Church. We profess therefore to be of the same society, and shall not walk answerably to our profession unless we employ ourselves in the same work.

2. Let it be considered that we all hope to spend an eternity with the saints in heaven, and in the same work of praising God. There is, it may be, not one of us but who hopes to be a saint in heaven, and there continually to sing praises to God and the Lamb. But how disagreeable will it be with such a hope to live in the neglect of praising God now! We ought now to begin that work which we intend shall be the work of another world; for this life is given us on purpose that therein we might prepare for a future life. The present state is a state of probation and preparation—a state of preparation for the enjoyments and employments of another, future, and eternal state—and no one is ever admitted to those enjoyments and employments but those who are prepared for them here. If ever we would go to heaven, we must be fitted for heaven in this world; we must here have our souls molded and fashioned for that work and that happiness. They must be formed for praise, and they must begin their work here. The beginnings of future things are in this world. The seed must be

sown here; the foundation must be laid in this world. Here is laid the foundation of future misery and future happiness. If it is not begun here, it never will be begun. If our hearts are not in some measure tuned to praise in this world, we shall never be anything at the work hereafter. The light must dawn in this world or the sun will never rise in the next. As we therefore, all of us, would be, and hope to be, of that blessed company who praise God in heaven, we should now inure ourselves to the work.

3. Those works of God's mercy for which the saints in heaven will chiefly praise Him have been wrought among us in this world.

The mercy and grace of God for which the saints in heaven will chiefly praise Him is His mercy exercised in the work of redemption, which work has been wrought out in this world. This love of God is the chief object of their admiration, and what they chiefly contemplate, and that employs their most ardent praises.

The grace of Christ about which their praises will be principally employed is that He should so love sinful man as to undertake for him, to take upon Himself man's nature, and to lay down His life for him. We find that is the subject of their praises in Revelation 5:8-9: "And when He had taken the book, the four living creatures and the four and twenty elders fell down before the Lamb, having every one of them harps, and golden vials full of odors, which are the prayers of saints. And they sang a new song, saying, 'Thou art worthy, for Thou has redeemed us to God by Thy blood.'"

They will chiefly praise God for these fruits of His mercy, because these are the greatest fruits of it that ever have been—far greater than the glorifying of saints. The saints in heaven will praise God for bestowing glory upon them; but the actual bestowment of glory upon them, after it has been purchased by the blood of Christ, is in no measure so great a thing as the purchasing of it by His blood. For Christ, the eternal Son of God, to become man and lay down His life was a far greater thing than the glorifying of all the saints who ever have been or ever will be glorified, from the beginning of the world to the end of it. Giving Christ to die comprehends all other mercies; for all other mercies are through this. The giving of Christ is a greater thing than the giving of all things else for the sake of Christ. This evidently appears from Romans 8:32: "He who spared not His own Son, but delivered Him up for us all, how shall He not with Him also freely give us all things?" So that the work of redemption is that for which the saints in heaven chiefly praise God. But this work has been wrought here among us in this world. "The Word was made flesh, and dwelt among us." The incarnation of Christ was a thing that was brought to pass in this world, and the sufferings and death of Christ were also accomplished on earth. Shall heaven be filled with praises for what was done on earth, and shall there be no praises on earth where it was done?

4. If you praise God sincerely in this world, it will be a sign that you are really to be one of those who shall praise Him in heaven. If any man is found sincerely glorifying God, he will in due time be brought to them as one who is fit to be of their company. Heaven is the appointed place of all sincere praisers of God; they are all to be gathered together there. And no man can sincerely praise God unless he is one of those who are redeemed from among men, one whom God has separated from the rest of the world and set apart for Himself.

5. If we begin now to exercise ourselves in the work of heaven, it will be the way to have foretastes of the enjoyments of heaven. The business and the happiness go together. This will be the way to have your heart filled with spiritual joy and

comfort. If you heartily praise God, you shall rejoice in Him, and He will show you more of Himself, of His glory and love, that you may still have greater cause of praise.

I proceed to give some directions for the performance of this work.

1. Be directed, in order to your acceptably performing this duty, to repent of your sins and turn to God. If you have not a work of conversion wrought in you, you will do nothing to any purpose in this work of praise. An unconverted person never once sincerely or acceptably praises God. If you would do the work of the saints in heaven, you must be not only in profession, but really, one of their society; for there are none else who can do their work. As in the verse following the text: "And they sang as it were a new song before the throne, and before the four living creatures, and the elders; and no man could learn that song but the hundred and forty-four thousand which were redeemed from the earth." A hundred and forty-four thousand is a mystical number for the Church of God, the assembly of the saints, or those who are redeemed from the earth. There is no man who can learn the song that they sing in heaven but those of that number. It is beyond the reach of all natural men, let them be persons of ever so great abilities and sagacity. They never can learn that heavenly song if they are not of that number. For it is only the sanctifying, saving instruction of the Spirit of God that can teach us that song.

2. Labor after more and more of those principles from whence the praise of the saints in heaven arises. You have already heard that the saints in heaven praise the Lord so fervently because they see Him. Labor therefore that you, though you have not an immediate vision of God as they have, may yet have a clear spiritual sight of Him, and that you may

know more of God and have frequent discoveries of Him made to you.

You have heard that the saints in heaven make praise so much their work because of the great sense they have of the greatness and wonderfulness of the fruits of the Lord's goodness. Labor therefore to get your minds more deeply impressed with such a sense.

The saints in glory are so much employed in praise because they are perfect in humility, and have so great a sense of the infinite distance between God and them. They have a great sense of their own unworthiness, that they are by nature unworthy of any of the mercy of God. Labor therefore that you may obtain more of a sense of your own littleness and vileness; that you may see more what you are, how ill you have deserved at the hands of God, and how you are less than the least of all His mercies.

The hearts of the saints in heaven are all inflamed with divine love, which continually influences them to praise God. Seek that this principle may abound in you, and then you likewise will delight in praising God. It will be a most sweet and pleasant employment to you.

3. Labor in your praises to praise God so far as may be in the same manner as the saints do in heaven. They praise Him fervently with their whole heart, and with all their strength, as was represented in the vision to John by the exceeding loudness of their praise. Labor therefore that you may not be cold and dull in your praises, but that you also may praise God fervently.

The saints in heaven praise God humbly. Let it also be your delight to abase yourselves, to exalt God, to set Him upon the throne, and to lie at His footstool.

The saints in heaven praise God unitedly. They praise Him with one heart and one soul in a most firm union. Endeavor that you may thus praise God in union with His people, having your hearts knit to them in fervent love and charity, which will be a great help to your praising and glorifying God unitedly with them.

USE OF REPROOF:
Let this be a reproof to those who neglect the singing of God's praises. Certainly such a neglect is not consonant with the hope and expectation of spending an eternity in that work. It is an appointment of God that we should not only praise in our prayers, but that we should sing His praises. It was a part of divine worship not only under the Old Testament, but the New. Thus we read that Christ and His disciples sang praises together (Matthew 26:30). So it is commanded in Ephesians 5:18–19: "Be ye filled with the Spirit, speaking to yourselves in psalms and hymns and spiritual songs, singing and making melody in your hearts to the Lord." And Colossians 3:16: "Let the Word of Christ dwell in you richly in all wisdom; teaching and admonishing one another in psalms, and hymns, and spiritual songs, singing with grace in your hearts to the Lord." 1 Corinthians 14:15: "I will sing with the spirit, and I will sing with the understanding also." So also the saints in heaven are represented as singing God's praises. And is that their happy and glorious employment; and yet shall it be so neglected by us who hope for heaven? If there are any of the godly who neglect this duty, I would desire them to consider how discordant such a neglect is with their profession, with their state, and with the mercies which God has bestowed. How much cause has God given you to sing His praise! You have received more to prompt you to praise God than all the natural men in the world; and can you content yourself to live in the world without singing the praises of your heavenly Father, and your glorious Redeemer?

Parents ought to be careful that their children are instructed in singing, that they may be capable of performing that part of divine worship. This we should do as we would have our children trained up for heaven; for we all would have our children go to heaven.

USE OF CONSOLATION TO THE GODLY:
It may be matter of great comfort to you that you are to spend your eternity with the saints in heaven, where it is so much their work to praise God. The saints are sensible of what cause they have to praise God, and oftentimes are ready to say that they long to praise Him more, and that they never can praise Him enough. This may be a consolation to you, that you shall have a whole eternity in which to praise Him. The saints earnestly desire to praise God better. This, therefore, may be your consolation, that in heaven your heart shall be enlarged; you shall be enabled to praise Him in an immensely more perfect and exalted manner than you can do in this world. You shall not be troubled with such a dead, dull heart; with so much coldness, so many clogs and burdens from corruption, and from an earthly mind; with a wandering, unsteady heart; with so much darkness and so much hypocrisy. You shall be one of that vast assembly that praises God so fervently that their voice is "as the voice of many waters, and as the voice of mighty thunderings."

You long to have others praise God, to have everyone praise Him. In that place there will be enough to help you and join you in praising Him, and those who are capable of doing it ten thousand times better than saints on earth. Thousands and thousands of angels and glorified saints will be around you, all united to you in the dearest love, all disposed to praise God not only for themselves, but for His mercy to you.